CONTENTS

ACKNOWLEDGMENTS

Each of us has a special sort of appreciation for the members of our families, an appreciation for being engaged in a strange and rewarding process of being related to one another. In this, we include those family members who are absent, deceased or abandoned to the care of others. Thanks to: our partners, Scott and Jim, who continue to support us through project after project after project; mentors, Marion S. and Pam M., for unconditional love through a difficult turning point; and to Vern S., for strengthening of skills in thought. Thanks also to: Dave L., who opened his heart and his home to this project and the editorial and publishing wizards who saw it through at Health Communications, Inc. Finally, we'd like to thank each other, for the creativity, friendship and hard work that have gone into the incredible process of writing this book: we've come to understand partnership far better and to love each other more.

We join in appreciation toward all of you who have cheered us and loved us. You all know who you are. And to "our friends we haven't yet met," we extend to you, "welcome!" May rainbows and silver bells light and cheer your days; may you find your "pots of gold" (whatever they may be) and may you be blessed with contentment.

Kathleen W. and Jewell E.
Eureka, California

INTRODUCTION

Because many support groups for Adult Children in recovery are already in existence and others are in the process of being formed, we decided to create this 12-Step guide, or workbook, to provide an important middle ground between traditional 12-Step literature and workshop-oriented therapies.

One reason we feel such a workbook is needed is because many Adult Children's 12-Step recovery programs have an open literature policy, encouraging their members to explore any books, therapies or spiritual practices that the individual finds helpful in reparenting the Inner Child. With many approaches, theories and methods available to recovering Adult Children, this guide offers new insights in the trusted process of "working the Steps", and thus, may serve to reduce confusion or friction over such questions as, "Which method, book or therapy is *best?*"

Competition between various authorities is an old, familiar tune to which most Adult Children learned to dance the "dysfunctional waltz" in their childhood. Stress over whether or not one point of view is more spiritual than another or more accepted is likely to create division in a group and rekindle feelings of fear or rebellion in individuals. We are convinced that a better way involves embracing new methods and approaches to health, which we then bring to the reliable process of recovery, the 12-Step programs.

Similarly, for those attending support groups that have

authorized or official literature, this workbook's middle-of-the-road approach offers motivated members a way to integrate their outside reading and personal work with the 12-Step program point of view on a personal basis, without encountering the resistances that somtimes arise over issues of outside literature at meetings.

For those who have not yet joined a support group, this workbook offers a way to become generally familiar with the Steps as a *process* to be used day by day, and integrated into a more positive style of living as they work the various exercises and practice the skills taught in the "Tools".

Adult Children who are parents themselves will find this workbook helpful in introducing recovery concepts to young children in the home where it may not be possible or desirable to take them to support groups.

Whether shared with friends or used independently, this workbook is designed to familiarize the reader with the 12 Steps of Recovery so that the good habits of this recovery process can increasingly become natural responses to stresses, issues and concerns as they arise.

Poem For Hannah, Maggy And Bob

They were waiting on the westwind
by the side of the river . . .
several tousle-haired kids and a smiling gold dog . . .
panting and stretching while the sky moved by . . .
. . . clouds like small sailboats on a very great pond
I remember what Sandy said about his poor mother:
that it wasn't God would pay all the bills!
it was all up to her . . .
while the sky moved along toward the glaring gold sunset
I wondered if all adults just never had time
I decided right then that I would get older — and I
wouldn't ever grow up
with a world on my shoulders
and a sky full of boats all sunk in the night sky . . .
Westwind brought the taste of woodburning smoke
as the golden dog stretched and Sandy got up
to go help out with dinner
I was ready to throw a rock after him
and his mother who really does run the world
and God had nothing to do with it . . . !
Mosquitoes and fish beginning to jump
while the westwind is sweet with the smell
of our dinner . . .
cooking in timelessness
where yellow dogs and tousle-haired kids
have nothing to do with it . . .
watching the cloud boats
sail away on the dreams
of my childhood.

Raven
(October 8, 1987)

1 WHY STUDY THE 12 STEPS OF RECOVERY?

Issues change. *Interests* may also change, and even thoughts and feelings change or become transformed. As Adult Children grow and recover from their patterns of dysfunction, the 12 Steps of Recovery provide a reliable *process* and a source of continuity that has universal appeal.

Whether atheist, church member or "New Age" experimenter, the 12 Steps offer the *spiritual* support of fellowship to those who adopt them. Tolerance and unconditional love remain the watchwords of all 12-Step support groups. These support groups are organized by volunteers and are open to those who identify with a broad range of personal issues.

Individuals, moving at their own pace with the 12 Steps, are encouraged to address the issues they choose and to chart their own course and direction. At the same time, *isolation* yields to *identification* and loneliness is replaced by feelings of belonging.

The 12 Steps offer an effective framework for personal growth — flexible, secure and time-tested. Simple to learn and powerfully effective in the lives of those who practice them, the 12 Steps provide the common ground where all who seek may find a path to personal contentment.

2 WHY CHOOSE A 12-STEP SUPPORT GROUP?

In recent years, much new scientific and spiritual awareness has developed supporting the principles of gradualness and of reinforcement through identification and interaction with a peer support group — the basic tenets of the 12-Step programs. Ideas of self-care that entailed more or less handing one's self over to the care of an *external* specialist, whether medical, psychological or spiritual, have largely been abandoned in favor of concepts that involve consciously joining in our own healing, clearing and empowering. Just as alcoholics working with each other in the original 12-Step Program of Alcoholics Anonymous (AA) empowered each other, as each connected with her own unique source of personal power ("God as we understand . . ."), more and more medical, psychological and spiritual opinion supports this process of "going within" as a vital ingredient in healing and wholeness.

As our understanding of the physiology of the brain increases, we are beginning to understand that mental and emotional wholeness also include a **physical element** and **process**, not just conceptual or spiritual ideals.

The right-left division of the human brain indicates that such functions as speech, "cause and effect" analytic thinking and sequential events or activities are governed (in most people) by the left hemisphere of the cerebral cortex; whereas the right hemisphere functions in largely nonverbal images, pattern recognition, and associations of memories, possibilities and imagination that are timeless in nature.

The intercommunication of the brain's hemispheres is accomplished through a vast network of nerves known as the corpus callosum. This network connecting the two hemispheres seems vital to creativity, vivid insights and intelligence.

Because young children have developed few skills in the left hemisphere, such as analytic thinking abilities or verbal skills and habits, it seems likely that much of the early patterning associated with growing up in alcoholic or dysfunctional families occurs in the right hemisphere or imaginative side of our physical minds. This patterning, for the most part, is not accessible through the analytical activities made possible in the left hemisphere.

Thus, recovery for Adult Children may include developing methods to contact the earlier images, sensations and feeling lodged in the right hemisphere of the brain, and coaxing them into conscious communication through the left hemisphere's abilities to speak and reason.

We literally may be engaged in healing the internal communications of the physical brain within ourselves as we metaphorically become whole in our lives and in our hearts!

Some research indicates that the survival of human beings depends on such left hemisphere coping skills as rational thinking (rationalizing), speech, and keeping track of time and sequences of events. When we are faced with stressful conditions, this dependency tends to cause the shutdown of intercommunication between the two hemispheres of the brain and to restrict the normal flow of images and pattern associations from the right side in favor of more analytical, linear thinking of the left side. Thus, emotions, which are largely experienced through the function of the right side of the brain, become suppressed.

If this mechanism operates in an adult, the "cool-headedness" or ability to make quick decisions that many of us have experienced under sudden stress may indeed be a valuable survival tool or a "mental edge" for humanity.

However, if the brain's normal right-left hemisphere interchange and flow are habitually and chronically blocked, serious interference might well occur to normal emotional and mental development. Such extreme stress conditions prevailing in early childhood that might adversely thwart this normal interchange and flow include the fearful, threatening conditions of an alcoholic or a dysfunctional home environment.

A characteristic of Adult Children, described as "becoming addicted to excitement", may represent a maladaptation of this survial mechanism. Infants or young children in dysfunctional/alcoholic homes who are prematurely, repeatedly and chronically exposed to conditions of violence or threat (conditions that would not be present in healthy families) may neurologically accept crisis as normal. This acceptance produces tendencies that some Adult Children experience as shutting down emotionally or overreacting involuntarily to *any* stress in the form of anxiousness, defensiveness or evasiveness.

Thus, our efforts in reparenting ourselves may include reestablishment of physical intercommunications within our own brains. These connections may not have been fully developed or may have been inappropriately developed because of our own physiological self-protective mechanisms, and now need to be renegotiated from within, as we act as our own protective, loving parents. The Tools included in this workbook are designed to support these levels of internal renegotiation. *Realistic* self-trust and self-responsibility are given time to develop, within the basic structure and spirit of 12-Step programs for healing.

As we move gradually to contact and nurture our lost Inner Child, we can incorporate the long successful history of the 12-Step program methods. Much of what the 12-Step programs advocate seems to be effective in dealing with addictive/compulsive/phobic personalities. The methods of gradualness, repeated contact, support from peers and identification with others similarly affected, seem to be supported and validated by scientific research and studies. The readily available peer support groups provide a safe and trustworthy setting for personal healing when combined with the Tools included here, which are designed to meet the needs and requirements of Adult Children of alcoholic/dysfunctional families.

In 12-Step programs, practical success is paramount. The goal for individuals is effective, joyful living. We do welcome new insights, understandings and validation of research, but theoretical knowledge is not an end in itself. A key to continuing success for the individual and for the method itself is the ability to remain open to new information and applications for achieving personal healing and well-being.

We look at what has worked well for us in the past, and we keep doing it. Working on a one-day-at-a-time basis, we also strive to improve and adapt our own goals, dreams and desires. The Adult Children's 12-Step programs thus remain live and vital forces for growth in a living universe.

3 APPLYING THE 12 STEPS TO PATTERNED BEHAVIOR

As newcomers to Adult Children support groups are introduced to the 12 Steps, often questions arise as to how the Steps apply to personal issues. The motivations that bring most of us to recovery are repeated experiences of feeling trapped in patterns of loneliness and self-defeat or being blocked and unable to contact one's own identity or to feel true feelings. What do the 12 Steps have to do with breaking these patterns, patterns which most experts agree are at the central core of our dysfunction?

We may have read enough to understand that the application of effective tools for releasing ourselves from these reactions, phobias and compulsions is, in the simplest terms, the test of recovery. But many of us were only dimly aware (if we could see at all) of what our patterned behaviors were. The prospect of having to dig, pry and scrape away old painful experiences and then fit them into the strange new system of these mysterious Steps, just to be able to talk about our problems, seemed pretty overwhelming, if not simply impossible. We need to feel better *now*. Is learning this new system of the 12 Steps worth the bother?

Because the Steps have such a great track record of success in supporting individuals in their recoveries from **active**

alcoholism and many other addictions that were once thought to be hopeless, beyond medical, psychological or even spiritual aid, we are encouraged to try the same principles of the 12 Steps on the dysfunctional patterned behaviors encountered in Adult Children. These patterned behaviors are seen to be very similar to the addictive patterns of alcoholism or substance abuse, even though the Adult Child may not drink. Those who have attempted the 12-Step process as a means of dispersing patterned behaviors arising from childhood experiences relate that they have found genuine relief from patterns they once may have feared were hopeless. We *suggest* the Steps, because they seem to be effective and because the changes seem to be potentially permanent.

By patterned behaviors we mean the ugly experiences of being used, rejected, abandoned or betrayed by others, and being caught in the ruts and routines that continually emerge from ourselves. Usually we cannot directly see the behaviors in question until they've led us down the predictable path characterized by running, "shutting down", "blowing up", "falling apart", "going nuts", getting jealous or critical and losing interest.

Any behavior that happens *repeatedly* in our lives and that prevents intimacy, continuity or physical/emotional security may be seen as this sort of patterned behavior. This behavior renders us dysfunctional in satisfying our own most basic human needs and desires.

In Adult Children support groups, members are encouraged to develop a personal program using the 12 Steps of Recovery. This, along with therapy, religious or self-development practices, or nutritional/medical support they find attractive, helps them to *reparent* themselves by replacing patterned behaviors with an ability to make choices and decisions.

Adult Children support groups remain firmly centered in the 12-Step process and in the sharing that takes place at meetings. This group sharing tends to support trust, both in the group and in each member's own experience. As trust and confidence grow, buried memories and "stuffed" feelings tend to surface into consciousness. This group aspect of the

12-Step program process is an important element in reducing individual isolation and feelings of uniqueness.

For the newcomer, however, applying the Steps of Recovery raises such questions as:

1. Just how do I eliminate incidents that happened in the distant past?
2. If those incidents are the cause of my present reactions, phobias and compulsions, am I supposed to inventory the past where it all started or the here and now?
3. While I'm going through this digging and self-reflection, do I just stop living, until I get it all straightened out and clear?
4. How will I know when I'm well enough to avoid repeating the dysfunction?
5. If I find myself making the same mistakes, am I a failure and is there really no hope for me?

Ultimately, of course, each person answers his own questions. It has been our experience that using the inventory process on both the past basic cause of events that affected us so deeply in our childhood as well as inventorying our current reactions breaks long-established barriers of denial. Once this practice is enacted it tends to free us in the present from overreaction, projection or getting "hooked" into other people's dysfunctional tapes.

It is essential to have a genuinely personal sense of the Steps as a process with continuity and meaning in order to recognize a patterned behavior and then to move from reacting to taking inventory. This new knowledge can be compared to learning to ride a bike. Once it is integrated, it then ceases to be awkward and mechanical and becomes a source of personal power. **This goal of personal integration of the 12 Steps of Recovery is the focus of this guide.**

Specifically, the tools and exercises are selected and designed to work *with* the Steps, calling on many levels, such as thinking mind, imagination plus Inner Child and other inner personalities (some of whom may be new in your experience).

You may question or reject the use of such spiritual terms and concepts as either unreal or in conflict with established ideas you may hold about spirituality or God. This is perfectly all right. Most find that simply doing the Exercises in the spirit of "let's pretend" is ample credibility to prompt the imagination to reveal previously locked and barred areas within ourselves — often through vividly enriched dreams.

Healing begins as the self feels, dreams, recalls sense memories, integrates the 12 Steps and unlocks our buried memories. We let ourselves feel as we continue to think, encouraging ourselves to become all that we can be as healthy human beings. Over a period of time, we gain in power and freedom, thus experiencing ". . . a spiritual awakening as result of these Steps."

4 WORKING THE 12 STEPS OF RECOVERY

The 12 Steps of Recovery originated with Alcoholics Anonymous (AA) and were first published in 1939, in the AA *Big Book*. Since that beginning, many additional support groups have come into existence. With the permission of Alcoholics Anonymous World Service Organization, these groups use the same 12 Steps on other issues, adapting the wording to reflect the focus of the group. For those who are already members of 12-Step support groups, working the 12 Steps of Recovery may be a familiar process.

However, working the Steps on Adult Children's issues differs from applying the same Steps to an issue of active alcoholism or drug abuse. In Adult Children's support groups, lost or distorted personal identity issues are the focus of the Steps. The goal is to reparent that lost or injured inner self rather than to advocate abstinence from alcohol, drugs, food, etc. In Adult Children's support groups, the focus is on finding or restoring our childhood innocence and good health. This difference of orientation puts a new light on the process of working the 12 steps.

Several new textbooks have been published that deal specifically with applying the 12 Steps to various Adult Children's issues *(see Healing A Broken Heart, 12 Steps of*

Recovery for Adult Children, by Kathleen W., Health Communications, Inc., 1988). In some communities, special meetings exist to read, discuss and/or write about the Steps, utilizing one or more of these newer works and sometimes along with one of the old standards on the Steps (AA's or Al-Anon's *12 Steps and 12 Traditions*).

This workbook may be used as an independent guide or as a supplement with any other Step study work. The Tools and exercises included are designed to intensify the inventory processes involved in the Steps and to expand options in such areas as finding a personal Higher Power, or making amends. Also included are seven different approaches to the 12 Steps that can be combined with other reading, discussion or these Tools and exercises, as deemed appropriate or attractive.

The simple goal in recovery remains personal healing. "Doing it right" means *getting well.* There are no wrong ways to work the 12 Steps because in an evolving universe, new understanding continuously combines with what is tried and true.

Personal recovery means hearing and trusting the guidance from within and finally, becoming courageous enough to act from that truth. Integrating the 12-Step process is one way to become the master of that truth.

5 EXERCISES ON THE 12 STEPS

A 12-Step Outline For Busy People

Read the Steps, one by one, and ask yourself these questions. See if one, more than another, applies to you personally. If you like, change or add to the questions, but don't dwell on any one. You can return to those with special importance after you've surveyed them all.

1. **We admitted we were powerless over [the effects of] alcohol [or other dysfunctional behavior] — that our lives had become unmanageable.**
   Are there behaviors you feel powerless over, whether or not you see them as effects of alcoholism? As a consequence, is your life unmanageable, because you can't seem to avoid certain patterns, ruts and fear or rage reactions?
2. **Came to believe that a Power greater than ourselves could restore us to sanity.**
   What power, if any, do you trust? Is there a hopeless, empty confused feeling when you ask yourself this question? Does the idea of calling yourself insane frighten you, or make you angry?
3. **Made a decision to turn our will and our lives over to the care of God *as we understand God*.**

What feelings arise when you read this Step? Do any of these key ideas, "decision", "turn [your] will and [your] life over", "God", evoke strong reactions or images for you — perhaps from your past?

4. **Made a searching and fearless moral inventory of ourselves.**

   Do you have a guilty secret, crimes, sex-behavior or do you have secret fantasies of love or revenge? Are you in touch with your feelings? Can you identify them and recognize them for what they represent?

5. **Admitted to God, to ourselves and to another human being the exact nature of our wrongs.**

   What do you fear that God, as you understand God, won't forgive? What are you afraid to tell *anyone* about yourself? What isn't important enough to bother with or to share? Whom do you know who accepts you just as you are?

6. **Were entirely ready [and willing] to have God remove all these defects of character.**

   What old behaviors that used to serve you don't work any more and are now really in your way? If you let them go and stop doing them, what might happen? Is it worth the risk?

7. **Humbly asked God to remove our shortcomings.**

   Concentrate on breathing into your solar plexus (the area just below your diaphragm) and let go. Feel how it feels. Take another breath. Let yourself feel.

8. **Made a list of all persons we had harmed, and became willing to make amends to them all.**

   Who let you down? Who hurt you? Who taught you to be a victim, and with whom have you perpetuated this victim syndrome? Is there someone you can't forgive or someone you can't forget?

9. **Made direct amends to such people wherever possible, except when to do so would injure them or others.**

   Coming from love what action can you take now to heal or repair the past? Is the timing right?

10. **Continued to take personal inventory and when we were wrong promptly admitted it.**

Acknowledge your feelings right now. Today review and notice how you have felt. Have you been "stuffing" any feelings? Feel those now. Have you been imprisoned in childhood reactions? If you have, reevaluate these reactions in Step 1, when you have time . . . .

11. **Sought through prayer and meditation to improve our conscious contact with God *as we understand God*, praying only for knowledge of God will for us and the power to carry that out.**

    Is "prayer" a word with meaning for you? Do you feel you can meditate? What does "conscious contact" feel like? Is "knowledge of God's will" something you sense inside yourself? How about "power"?

12. **Having had a spiritual awakening as a result of these steps, we tried to carry this message to others, and to practice these principles in all our affairs.**

    What is a "spiritual awakening" in your life? Do you feel you "carry the message" in ways that are honestly "you"? Are there aspects of your life that your program presently does not address?

Working The Steps: An In-Depth Approach

After reading through the Steps and reflecting on them with the questions, choose the Step that seems most significant and write about it. Go over the *Victim/Freedom Wheels*, Tool I, with this Step as a focus. Try using the *Guided Visualization/ Active Imagination* process in Tool II to reflect within or on your questions or issues in this Step. Work several exercises with the Step, selecting exercises that seem appropriate. Allow yourself to explore.

Give yourself a time schedule — a week, a few hours, even a month — to explore this Step. Work with it until you feel an inner sense of completion. Take all the time you need. Reparent yourself with *gentlesness, humor and love.*

Another Approach: A Way To Break Up Denial

Try working the Step that seems least important. This is an

especially good idea if, after awhile in recovery, you notice that there are some Steps you *never* feel drawn to tackling. Use different exercises, too, to shift your focus and overcome your blind spots.

Design A Routine: A Personal Program

It's up to you to modify the Steps for your own use. For example, many people find comfort and security in taking a special time each day to meditate, pray or read in support of their own recovery. If you notice that you are using the first three Steps every day as a way to gain serenity before the flurry of daily events begins, adapt that practice and routine as part of your own personal program.

Perhaps you may find you use Step 11, not necessarily on your knees, but during the time you take to jog, to exercise or to wait in traffic on the drive to and from work. Give yourself credit for your spiritual work, in whatever way you are able to do it.

A personal development program is just that — personal, individual and unique. Development is a process that moves, changes and adapts. As we unburden ourselves from our pasts, we become freer and more in tune with our inner direction. Try designing different ways to use some of the Steps and see how your program works for a month. Then evaluate it and make the changes necessary to take you in a direction you'd like to go.

Begin At The Beginning: Working The Steps In Order

Many find less confusion by working through the Steps in order, giving a few weeks to each Step, meeting with a sponsor or therapist regularly, and/or sharing with a few contacts or in the group as they progress. The Steps can be covered by working alone; however, Steps 5 through 9 and Step 12 involve leaving isolation and interacting with people. Give yourself permission to take the necessary time and personal effort to build the required basis of trust that makes these interactions possible and ultimately comfortable. Don't rush or compete, but *do* continue. Try to become more sensitive to your own needs and requirements for support that do not stifle or intimidate.

In Step 12, we are asked to ". . . practice these principles [the Steps] in all our affairs." It is important to notice and acknowledge how and when we incorporate the perspectives we gain as the Steps become more familiar in our daily interactions. Noticing and acknowledging counteract the tendency many of us have to minimize or discount our own efforts and achievements.

For example, are you realizing what is beyond your control and admitting it *[Step 1]* instead of struggling in vain against impossibilities? Do you find that you're "letting go and letting God" *[Step 3]* in situations that used to unsettle you? Are you speaking up *[Step 5]* rather than stuffing? Do you let recovery get in *[Step 7]*? Are you taking personal times-out *[Step 11]*?

If you can't answer these questions affirmatively, you can use this insight as a guide to areas of your own program needing further concentration.

Also try to notice which Steps demand attention as you work with the Tools and issue exercises in later sections of this book. Remember; *you are* the *central figure* in your own recovery, and it is up to you to reflect and notice how . . . all [your] affairs . . . are involved in the practice and process.

"No Kidding Around": Working The Steps In One-Half Hour

1. What's the problem?

2. What can help?

3. Will I let it?

4. What do I know/feel about it?

5. Tell somebody (phone or person).

6. What do I want instead?

7. Keep an open mind/heart.

8. Who hurt me and who am I hurting?

9. Heal it, if possible.

10. How do I *feel,* right now?

11. Am I spiritually *centered*?

12. *How* is the program alive in me?

6 NEW TOOLS FOR WORKING THE 12 STEPS OF RECOVERY

In the tradition of successful 12-Step programs, we have created three Tools that embody three basic principles of recovery: *H*onesty, *O*pen-mindedness, and *W*illingness (the *HOW* of Alcoholics Anonymous recovery). Each Tool is presented with exercises designed to demonstrate several alternative ways to use the Tools, including ways to apply each of them to the 12 Steps.

Tool I

Tool I consists of two centering devices, the *Victim Roles Wheel* and the *Freedom Wheel.* These wheels are designed to encourage *H*onesty, bringing the focus of our thinking and understanding back on ourselves, rather than on the behaviors of others. Each. wheel contains a number of **behaviors** (or **affirmations**) that tend to feed and to support each other. First, they keep us bound and tied to Victim Roles and partnerships. Then, as denial loses power in our lives, they act as paired guideposts to greater freedom and markers on the path of self-honesty.

Tool II

Tool II is a **two-stage process** created especially to support Adult Children in Guided Visualization/Active Imagination techniques, including instructions for returning to peace and serenity as a safeguard that permits individual **pacing** and direction of these processes. Most find these dynamic processes, which are adaptations from the techniques of Dr. Carl Jung (an early psychologist), to be extremely helpful in contacting deep, sometimes painful, but often spiritual and creative aspects from within. These tools truly **open our minds!**

Tool III

Tool III, involving *Creative Action Routines,* offers practical suggestions for moving newly found (or long-held) insights from theory into *action!* Willingness to take action so that recovery becomes a reality is the goal of these techniques, which are actual applications of acting and communications skills selected to support self-exploration and expression, rather than to mask or to disguise inner needs or feelings.

These Tools can be used in any order. Therapists and fellowship peer-support groups may wish to focus on one or another of these techniques, perhaps creating workshops or setting up a special purpose meeting that focuses on one Tool, or uses each of them in order, over a period of weeks or months. Exercises included after each Tool lend themselves to being used in group workshops or for topics of discussion. Most may be used interchangeably with all three Tools and all 12 Steps.

Each of these Tools is designed to help uncover early memories. At the same time they will preserve the element of choice as to pace, depth and duration of the work so that each individual may move with greater security in the struggle to dispel denial.

Some therapies and spiritual practices that successfully break down barriers of denial may tend to leave us feeling somewhat out of control. With this concern in mind, these techniques are set up to permit anyone who chooses to do so to *step back* mentally and emotionally, *without* having to interrupt his healing process.

Because Adult Children deal with issues and behaviors that often have their roots in infancy and early childhood, much of what we need to examine may lie buried. We do indeed recover by taking responsibility for our actions in the present, but we usually need time and support to get in touch with the truth of our own histories!

The 12-Step principles of gradualness of repeated contact, identification and obtaining peer-support are respected here. For people like ourselves, perhaps most victimized by what may be concealed from our conscious awareness, this approach offers flexibility and room to grow.

We find that these Tools are strong and effective enough to open closed doors and turn on an internal light. Also, they're meant to be used gently, so that a fragile beginner Adult Child may risk the surfacing of feelings and memories, assuring an acceptable and reasonable pace of recovery/discovery rather than being swept into a turbulent whirlpool.

Using these Tools, creating time and making ourselves available to support are personal reparenting decisions. Adult children in recovery truly are people of great courage!

7 TOOL I: THE VICTIM ROLES WHEEL AND THE FREEDOM WHEEL

As Adult Children we may have resisted playing the victim roles when we were children, but we found that we just didn't have sufficient power to remain unaffected by our family pressures. We find ourselves infected, to a greater or lesser extent, with symptoms of the family disorder. Many of us find that we feel personal guilt and shame for family-based shortcomings.

". . . Living life from the standpoint of victims . . ." we have developed a self-protective practice of seeing more easily what the other person is doing to create victim roles, instead of accurately noticing and assessing our own behaviors. We may be concerned with others because we are all too uncomfortable looking at ourselves.

Victim Roles Wheel

In order to refocus on our own behaviors while realistically assessing our counterparts — such as parent figures, mates or co-workers with whom we are bonded in reaction — we have arranged dysfunctional characteristics on the Victim Roles Wheel, a centering device. (See Figure 7.1.)

23

Figure 7.1. Victim Roles Wheel*

(Acting-out Behaviors)   (Reactive Behaviors)

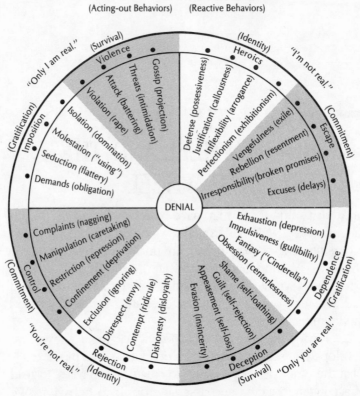

*©1987, EUREKA! Publishing.

Whether we are the type who sees ourselves constantly and pathetically in the wrong *(reactive behaviors)* or are more the type who picks apart our closest family members and friends *(acting-out behaviors)*, the Victim Roles Wheel gives us the chance to see all aspects of our past and current dilemmas. Each set of characteristics is located directly across the circle from its counterpart.

Each individual is equally a victim and a victimizer. Each one is seeking to satisfy a basic human need in ways that tend to limit, constrict or reduce both the self and the "significant other" in the process.

Though certain behaviors on the Victim Roles Wheel may appear more socially acceptable or more powerful, all fall into the category of victim and revolve around *denial.* Denial is the "central hub" of the Victim Roles Wheel, holding the various behavior "spokes" together in frustration and defeat.

An example of how one Victim Role can seem better than its counterpart might be that of a person who is always caring for others, never caring for herself. She appears to be the person engaging in more acceptable behavior than the person on the opposite spoke of the Wheel, who reacts with behaviors such as broken promises and irresponsibility. As we interpret it, both persons and behaviors are two spokes of the same wheel. The self-effacing caretaker is trying to control the promise breaker, who resists control and escapes.

Oddly enough, each person is relating from a basic human need for interpersonal *commitment* in this exchange, but each is doing so in ways that lead toward failure rather than mutual satisfaction. (See Figure 7.2.)

Figure 7.2. Victim Roles: Control versus Escape

(Acting-out Behaviors)   (Reactive Behaviors)

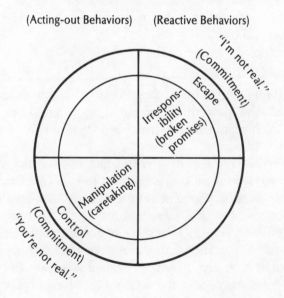

Notice that the promise breaker is not initiating, but instead is reacting contrary to what it may seem on the surface. Most caretakers believe they are helpless victims of irresponsible promise breakers, but it appears that willingness to caretake supports irresponsibility. These paradoxes make denial difficult to detect or dispel in family alcoholism/dysfunction.

As you examine the Victim Roles Wheel, notice how the paired behaviors interlock as spokes around a common *denial hub* that holds itself together and keeps rolling, making a powerful relationship for any two victims.

Many people act out these interlocking roles, limiting and constricting each other for long periods of time. If one person is very attached to staying on the Victim Roles Wheel, and her partner gets off the Wheel and recovers (or leaves or dies), she must recruit another with the right set of behaviors in order to keep the Victim Roles Wheel rolling. (It is the same story but with new names.)

"Living life from the standpoint of victims . . ." on the Victim Roles Wheel indicates the following attitudes:

1. Refusal/inability to be who we are or to allow others to be who they are
2. Refusal/inability to be in the present or to deal with the real past
3. Sense of powerlessness
4. Lack of choice

As difficult as it may be to face these behaviors, especially those that have powerfully structured and limited our own lives, this self-examination remains a necessary starting point in recovery/discovery.

The First Step in the 12-Step Program of Recovery states: "We admitted we were powerless over the effects of alcohol — that our lives had become unmanageable." Looking at the paired spokes of Victim Roles, which effects of alcohol have had us spinning, powerless and out of control? With personal recovery as our goal, how can we reorient and free ourselves?

Most of us have tried a number of methods to get our lives "unstuck" before joining the fellowship. Much of what we tried may have focused on the other person, perhaps trying to change them. If that failed, we tried to select healthy people, people who wouldn't bring old, painful Victim Role behaviors into our lives again. Most of us found that these forms of change were not successful. Behaviors and patterns of painful isolation reemerged with distressing predictability, matching our own concealed distortions of ourselves.

The Victim Wheel helps us refocus on our attitudes/behaviors and offers us the much needed opportunity to deal with our own issues, which may have been obscured by our emphasis on the issues of others. The goal of Adult Children's programs, "keeping the focus on ourselves . . .", is our main hope for actually freeing ourselves.

Unless we release ourselves from our Victim Roles, any recasting of the opposite personalities will probably be only temporary solutions to our personal dilemmas. Though difficult to accept, the realization that we must do the changing remains a fundamental principle that gives personal recovery direction.

Freedom Wheel

The Freedom Wheel, another centering device, shows how we may become free, healthy, self-directed adults who are no longer prisoners of childhood reactions. The Freedom Wheel is made up of *affirmations for alternative behaviors* that are *expressive* or *responsive* (replacing *reactive* or *acting out* behaviors, in the Victim Roles). These alternative behaviors revolve around *honesty,* the hub of the Freedom Wheel. (See Figure 7.3.)

Further, the Freedom Wheel suggests antidotes to the limitations of Victim Roles in the form of affirmation concepts. Each spoke of the Victim Role Wheel has a counterpart on the Freedom Wheel to aid in achieving healthy and balanced perspectives of our real life options. Living life from a standpoint of health (not as a victim) directs us to attitudes such as:

1. Acceptance of self and others in the present
2. Sense of personal power and self-esteem
3. Spiritual awakening
4. Unlimited choices

Figure 7.3. Freedom Wheel*

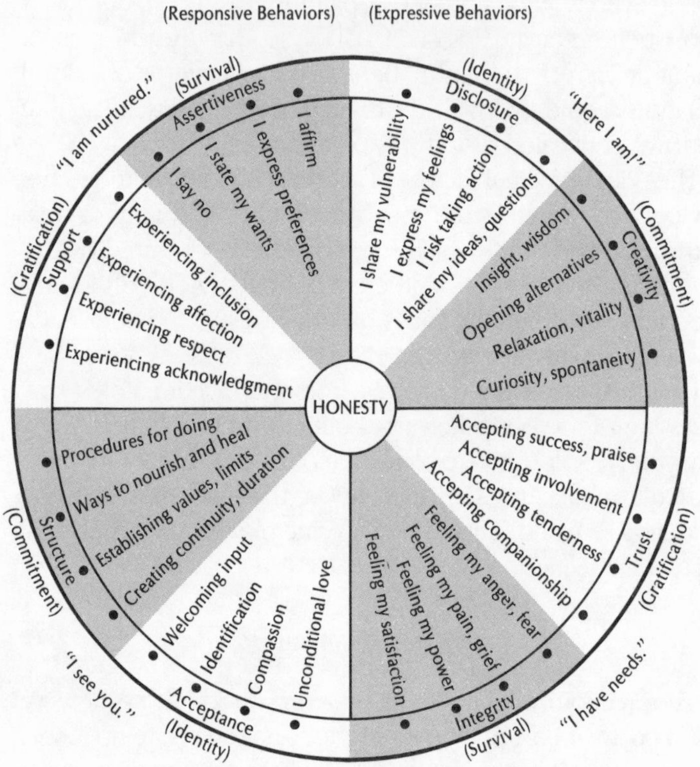

(Responsive Behaviors)   (Expressive Behaviors)

*©1987, EUREKA! Publishing.

To further amplify the illustration of the Victim Roles Wheel (p. 24), if the caretaker admits that (her) motive is to manipulate and control another in order to feel needed, then this honesty makes it possible to move to the Freedom Wheel's affirmative behaviors. (See Figure 7.2 and 7.4.)

Courage and honesty make possible the choices found on the Freedom Wheel. These choices were not previously available while the person was locked in the denial of the Victim Roles Wheel.

On the Freedom Wheel, the caretaker chooses the responsive behavior of introducing ways to nourish and to

Figure 7.4. Freedom: Structure versus Creativity

(Responsive Behaviors)   (Expressive Behaviors)

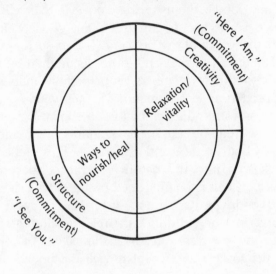

keep *commitment* in healthy and honest ways. Other persons are now free to accept or reject these alternatives without restrictions. Expression rather than reaction becomes an option. This expression encourages relaxation in others, which is a basis for healthy and voluntary commitment.

Contrasting The Victim Roles and Freedom Wheels

The basic human needs we are seeking to satisfy, on either of the Wheels, are referred to as *instincts* by Bill W. (*Step 4*, AA's Twelve Steps and Twelve Traditions). "Creation," he stated, "gave us instincts for a purpose. Without them we wouldn't be complete human beings."

We've adhered to Bill W.'s teachings. Viewing our behaviors as attempts to satisfy basic human needs has proven helpful in gaining a poised sense of ourselves. This outlook also encourages self-honesty because we can accept our inner drives as natural and good in themselves and not evils to be eliminated.

Science seems to support this point of view. Evidence suggests that much of our human behavior, such as children being parented, as mates and lovers, as mothers and fathers and as community members, is powerfully influenced or predisposed from deep nonrational centers within our brains. These areas within the cerebellum, medulla, hypothalamus and limbic regions are being examined with increasing interest by both medical and psychological researchers.

As research into the nature of Adult Children issues continues, insight is being gained on the ways these natural instinctive drives have been distorted by dysfunctional parenting in our childhoods. Creating alternatives that embrace these drives instead of eliminating or repressing them is the goal of these Wheels as well as a fundamental goal of reparenting ourselves in recovery.

We've taken a pragmatic approach and updated Bill W.'s terminology to reflect our present understanding and use of language: "an instinct for material-physical security" has been renamed *survival;* "social standing" we call *identity;* "emotional security" we term *commitment* and "sex-relations" we call *gratification.*

Each of these four basic drives, survival, identity, commitment and gratification appears twice on each Wheel opposite from one another. Beneath each pair, groups of four spokes make up characteristic behaviors that tend either toward satisfying the particular basic needs (Freedom) or toward limiting basic needs (Victim Roles).

Just inside the Wheels, in bold type, a general word describing the style or class of behavior involved in the four spokes is listed. For example:

1. Under survival on the Victim Roles Wheel, *violence* appears across from *deception.* Each is a class or style of behaviors that attempts to secure survival in a threatening and insecure world. On the Freedom Wheel, however, we find *assertiveness* across from *integrity* under survival, indicating styles of behaviors that tend to free us from threat, dangerous conditions and physical insecurity and move us to safer and saner environments.
2. Under identity, *disclosure* and *acceptance* on the Freedom Wheel replace old false fronts of *heroics* or painful blame-games of *rejection* that formerly characterized much of our experience in relating to ourselves and to others, either personally or socially.
3. Commitment, the need to sense connection to others and to life itself becomes *structure* or a process of limits and values to nourish and support. *Structure* is counterbalanced by *creativity,* which replaces old distortions of *control* and their inevitable counterparts in *escape.*
4. Under the term gratification, *imposition* or *dependence* (user-used characteristics of Victim Roles) are replaced by the affirmative concepts of *support* and *trust* (realizations of present internal resources). These new concepts move us toward a world where love and appreciation are freely given and happily received.

Try using the Wheels on issues or problems as they occur in your life and in connection with each of the 12-Steps as you refocus on yourself instead of others. The Freedom Wheel is helpful in circumventing blocks or blind spots where there seems to be a lack of choice or limited alternatives. Prepare affirmations for yourself from the Freedom Wheel to deal with issues on the Victim Roles Wheel that cause you difficulty. Use them in your practice of the Eleventh Step. Also, try using a spoke on the Freedom Wheel as an affirmation for meditation or prayer to aid in expanding your horizons.

Draw or trace these Wheels and put them where they are easy to see. This is helpful in gaining insight, sometimes unexpectedly, into your own motives and behaviors. The Wheels can be aids in seeing your relationship to yourself, to your own reactions in trying to control or manipulate yourself or to scare yourself.

Inner Tapes Exercise

Study the Victim Wheel, spoke by spoke. Listen to any inner tapes that you have and note any false, compulsive or fear-based messages you are presently sending to yourself. Toward the middle of your page write the phrase from the Victim Wheel spoke. Then list the deceptive messages to the side of each spoke.

Look at the counterpart spoke on the Freedom Wheel and write down the affirmation next to the Victim Wheel phrase. If you are able to do so, write down a "personal truth" about the affirmation that replaces the "old tape" for you. (See sample in Table 7.1 on p. 33.)

Creating With Affirmations

Affirmations are positive (and usually brief) statements based on concepts we understand to be true. Repeating a simple affirmation counteracts anxiety and fear of failure or of rejection, and helps keep our goals in focus.

Affirmations also may be used in prayer and meditation. They seem to be powerful unifiers, with the power to open channels in the heart and mind. It may be that they work to connect the subconscious and lower brain functions with the conscious mind, therefore tapping into latent resources from within. Most people who utilize affirmations notice an improvement in their personal attitudes and outlook on life.

A Basic Formula For Creating Affirmations

1. Notice (or admit) an area or issue in your life that is giving you trouble. To clarify your issues, study the

Table 7.1. Sample Inner Tapes Exercise

Lies	Victim Role	Freedom Wheel	Truths
I'm important because my appointment book is full.	Exhaustion (depression)	I accept praise!	I accept myself as a wonderful human being!
I'm awful. If anyone really knew me, they wouldn't like me.	Self-loathing (shame)	I feel my anger and my fear!	As a *whole* person, I experience anger and fear, and acknowledge them!
I don't fit in anywhere. I'm better, or worse, than others.	Exclusion (ignoring)	I welcome input!	I am a valuable person; I welcome input for my growth!
My way is the best way. My timetable is the most important.	Demands (obligations)	I experience feeling acknowledged!	I have valuable input to share, and I take pleasure in my effectiveness.
I need to win approval from others by flattery.	Seduction (flattery)	I experience feeling respected!	I am comfortable being who I am!

Victim Roles Wheel, and review any work you've done on Steps 1, 4 or 6.

Example: "I feel unworthy and undeserving," or "I'm depressed and I fear failure."

2. Consult the Freedom Wheel and select a concept that you feel is true but contradicts or replaces these negative ideas/feelings with a positive perspective.

Example: "I know I'm a human being, just like everyone else, and I, too, deserve happiness — just as I would wish success and happiness to anyone else," or "I accept that I can't expect to get anywhere in life, unless I try, however difficult that may be."

3. Put the concepts you mention in 2. in brief, direct and positive statements to yourself.

Example: "I deserve happiness — like everyone does." "Success depends on my taking action."

4. If you have a positive concept of God or of a Higher Power, add an element of this truth *(as you understand it)* to your affirmations.

Example: If your concept of God includes love, power or limitless creativity, incorporate these understandings in your affirmations by saying, "I am the beloved child of Limitless Spirit," "All my efforts are inspired by God's creative power," or "I accept the limitless power of God's love in my life and affairs today."

5. Without stuffing or denying your negative feelings or thoughts, say (or shout) your affirmations directly to the inner voices that are negating or condemning you, as though you are engaged in an argument.

Example: Old thoughts, such as "I can't do it," "No, my efforts aren't good enough," "My efforts are stupid," or "I really can't believe that," can be replaced with the affirmation that states, "All my efforts are inspired by God's creative power."

6. For persistent or especially painful negative thoughts or feelings, set aside 10-15 minutes per day for a two-week period to engage in this style of healing dialogue. If necessary, renew the commitment for additional periods of two weeks. Discuss your

stubborn issues with a sponsor or therapist *(Step 5)* and see if there is additional Step work you can do to clarify and dismiss these issues. Keep working until you *win* your inner debates and arguments.

7. Experiment creating affirmations that *stretch* the limits of what is possible for you, personally, financially, emotionally and spiritually. If you have any old dreams or forgotten goals in the recesses of your mind, revive them and aim for your highest level, using affirmations as your spiritual fuel.

Exercise Using The Victim Roles And Freedom Wheels In Tool I Along With Steps 1, 2 And 3

Choices

From experience I recognize that anytime I think I only have two choices and neither one of them feels quite right but rather is the lesser of two evils, I'm usually functioning from the Victim Roles Wheel.

When this happens, I surrender. This is one of the ways I work Steps 1, 2 and 3. In order to surrender to the wisdom of my Higher Power, I find it necessary to tell the truth. One aspect of truth that I can recognize is that I have a problem I feel I must solve; I can only come up with one or two choices and neither of these feels comfortable. In other words, I don't know a solution that suits me. I remind myself that it's okay to not know. Admitting that I don't know ("I'm powerless", *Step 1*) sends me to disclosure on the Freedom Wheel; this means I must admit who I am.

I complete my surrender by directing my disclosures to my Higher Power in prayer *(Steps 2 and 3)*. I may not always get solutions immediately through prayer, but by turning this over to my Higher Power I am *free* to take the focus off the problem (which I've admitted I can't solve right now). Then I go on to dealing with something I can do, like taking care of my immediate needs. For example, "Am I hungry or tired?" "Do I need to nurture myself in some way?" "Do I need to go to a meeting or to call someone?"

Therefore, I no longer find it necessary to vacillate between two ineffective choices and make myself crazy! From my experience in recovery, I now know that there are many choices that I cannot access from my old behavior patterns on the Victim Roles Wheel. I accept this and take Steps to surrender and become free.

An Exercise Using Tool I Wheels With The Serenity Prayer

Another technique to discover what lies I am telling myself that bind me to the Victim Roles Wheel, is to refer to the Serenity Prayer:

> God, grant me Serenity [calmness and peacefulness]
> To accept the things I cannot change [acquiescence]
> Courage to change the things I can [fortitude]
> And Wisdom to know the difference [guidance from a
> Higher Power].

I have divided this prayer into four parts: First, I come to a calm place and then, (referring to the situation I'm facing) I ask myself, "Is this a situation I am trying to control? Do I need to accept it instead? Or, is this a situation where I am assuming the role of victim (and, therefore, need to face it with increased courage)?" If I am unsure about what is going on or confused about which role I am playing, I postpone taking hasty action and seek wisdom/guidance from my Higher Power.

Example: Suppose someone owes me $100 for some work I did and I should have received the check in the mail at least three days ago. I really need the money for basic expenses and bills. My first thought is to call the person. I notice that I have told myself that it's okay for me to do something about the money because I need it, but not just because I worked for it and deserve it.

My next thought is to become afraid he'll be offended and suspect I don't trust him. Because he did express that he liked my work and I have the potential of more work from and through him, I don't want to offend him by pressuring him to pay. In a matter of about 60 seconds, I have managed to visualize this person as an authority figure whose reactions I feel threatened by (in the area of financial security). I've slipped onto the Victim Roles Wheel, under *deception, appeasement.* As I realize this, I acknowledge to myself that I have kept my commitments to this person, in the agreed time frame. He has not kept his word to me (though there may be an explanation), but my worry is that he might be offended!

I refer to the Serenity Prayer and ask: Is this a situation I can change (and just need to muster some courage)? Or is this a situation I cannot change (and, thus, need to exercise acceptance)? (If I had felt confused, enraged or helpless, I would have taken a prayer break until my Higher Power granted me wisdom.)

After a little reflection, I decide that it is my lack of courage to investigate about the money that is holding me a prisoner on the Victim Roles Wheel. The lie I'm telling myself appears to be something like, "His needs are more important than mine are," which locates me somewhere on the *"only you are real"* quadrant of the Victim Roles Wheel, centered either in (self-) *deception* or *dependence.*

To give myself courage, I consider the statements on the Freedom Wheel, particularly the statement that replaces *appeasement* with *feeling my power.* Realistically I consider how I have performed as agreed and when I am calm, I make the call.

He responds that he has mailed the check, but he would like me to stop by and estimate some more work if I am available. In this case, the truth and action of "Courage to change the things I can" shifted me to living from the Freedom Wheel experience.

I don't always get the result I hoped for when I'm operating from the Freedom Wheel. Sometimes it's an even better outcome. But, my chances are certainly greater from the Freedom Wheel perspective; plus, I always feel good about myself. I have my sense of integrity because I have been honest with myself and another person.

If I had felt manipulated in my communication with my employer, *assertive* spokes on the Freedom Wheel would have been the appropriate direction to follow in maintaining my own serenity, regardless of how manipulative or dishonest the other person may have been.

Examining this incident from the perspective of my recovery, I notice that the incident elicits childhood reactions. A flashback reaction occurred, where I experienced feeling "powerless" *(Step 1)* when I originally faced the issue of requesting prompt payment. Glimpses of memories — images and feelings — flashed before me as I moved through this experience. They took me back to the period of my life between the ages of 10 and 15 when I often felt exploited or taken advantage of by family members and others where work or money were concerned. I resolve to look over this period of my life, in working Step 4, reviewing and exploring the Victim Roles I assumed.

Assessing Shared Responsibility

Candice D., who shared this exercise with us, pointed out that many Adult Children are inclined to think in terms of black or white when it comes to assessing responsibility, eg., "It's *my* fault," or "It's *your* fault." Blaming, name-calling, or lying and concealing may be normal styles of assessing responsibility in much that we experience today, but these certainly are not healthy methods.

This exercise, Assessing Shared Responsibility, is a way to take an honest look at conflict or stress situations, taking into account holisticly factors of self, others and situations as they arise. With this approach, guilt and fear tend to subside and real problem solving becomes a greater possibility.

Use this exercise with the Victim Roles Wheel and the Freedom Wheel (Tool I) to determine how denial and honesty are contributing to the current status of events.

1. What is the problem, difficulty or aborted effort to be assessed? (Be as specific as possible and don't use name-calling or blaming in defining the problem.)

2. How did the *situation* contribute to the problem? (Consider factors such as: being jobless, being evicted, experiencing illness, abusing substances, etc.)

3. How did *others* contribute? (Specify people involved: work, family, etc.)

4. How did *I* contribute? (Consider self-criticism, self-examination, habits, weaknesses, etc.)

5. How have I handled similar issues *in the past?* (Notice any improvement and difference of perspective.)

6. How can I handle it now, to my best advantage? (Be realistic and fair to yourself!)

Guidelines To Be Considered As A Basis For Justice And Fairness In Relationships

1. Remember to ask for 100 percent of what you want in your relationships.
2. Don't do anything you really don't want to do.
3. Don't do more than 50 percent of the work (as you see it) in your relationships, be it physical, emotional, financial, sexual or spiritual.

8 TOOL II: GUIDED VISUALIZATION/ ACTIVE IMAGINATION

The admonition to "keep an open mind" is often heard around 12-Step support groups and is considered an essential ingredient in recovery. Many Adult Children will ask, "How can we keep our minds open, when many of us can remember only isolated incidents of *years* of our lives, especially our childhoods?" "How do you open a mind that is sealed shut?"

Others may have memories that haunt or torment them when they are recalled. They want to know if they must dredge up these painful, humiliating or revolting experiences in order to recover. Are we to relive horrors, feelings and experiences we've worked hard to suppress?

These questions are valid concerns to consider and support in recovery. Each group is more or less apprehensive about the *past*, feeling apprehensive about being open-minded with his personal history and experiences.

The Guided Visualization/Active Imagination process is an effective means to unlock closed mental doors while introducing previously untapped resources of personal spiritual power. Ultimately spiritual power heals us and dispels fears by opening doors of internal prisons that may have kept us from living life to the fullest.

Guided Visualization/Active Imagination empowers and centers inner identity and heals from within. From a base of greater personal strength, we become able to risk exploring painful histories and feelings.

The Jungian techniques employed in Guided Visualization/ Active Imagination are gentle, permissive, suggestive and supportive of feelings rather than directive or authoritarian in nature. These traits can overcome blocks by reducing fears and internal defensive reactions. As far as effective self-communication is concerned, permissive suggestion is an example of "less is more". This is especially true for those who have automatic defenses toward authority directives or resistance to taking orders.

Guided Visualization/Active Imagination practices have become widely accepted among body-workers, yoga and other meditation practitioners and religious groups that emphasize locating spiritual guidance from within. In addition, applications in psychology, hypnotherapy and accelerated learning programs may use these techniques for exploring past issues or replacing old habits with new alternatives. These potentially powerful applications may be useful in recovery/discovery, provided they respect the specific needs of Adult Children. These needs include: (1) personal empowerment and an enhanced sense of identity (stemming from lack of self-esteem) and (2) simple and effective ways to pace recovery. Adult Children need to go at their own pace in order to willingly risk painful, humiliating or revolting experiences from their traumatic childhoods.

Stage I: Visualization

Stage I of the two-stage process for Guided Visualization/ Active Imagination offers techniques to achieve healing, centering and gaining a sense of personal safety and confidence within ourselves. The goal of Stage I is to create an inner place of peace, sanctuary and inspiration, or a favorite place within ourselves where healing can occur.

In Stage I the healing may continue in spite of responsibilities of your job, children, school or personal relationships. The potential for this uninterrupted healing element is an important aspect of this process.

The Visualization practice can be used consciously to delve deeply and more sensitively into any of the 12 Steps or to strengthen contact with a Higher Power. For example, when used along with prayer and meditation in Step 11, the process tends to release buried memories and restore feelings that had been lost. This in turn clarifies the releasing of old behaviors and attitudes mentioned in Steps 4 and 6 through 9.

Stage II: Active Imagination

The combination of Active Imagination with Visualization from Stage I makes possible the reexamination of our personal histories as they exist within our own minds on a feeling level, making satisfying new adjustments in the process. From the place of security found in Stage I, we can undertake Stage II and venture deeper into self-exploration, encountering memories of figures and events. Here we can experience rescue and empowerment, and can rejoice with our Inner Child as we use our own unique resources for creative change.

In this two-stage application, each of us remains in charge and able to return comfortably to the Sanctuary of personal healing in Stage I. This may happen when time requires the focus be returned to other interests or responsibilities, or when we feel the need for more internal time to heal and to nurture ourselves.

The effects of Guided Visualization/Active Imagination practice vary, from person to person. Some experience sudden insight, new and brilliant light flooding issues that formerly may have been real puzzles. Others experience gradual, cumulative effects, subtle changes in perceptions, or new concepts and ideas for handling challenges in practical living. Most who have familiarized themselves with these techniques find that they do gain self-esteem from these practices and develop an enhanced realization of their own individual inner identity.

The final instruction, "Stepping back to Sanctuary", from Stage I applies to any point in Stage II, allowing for individual progress at a relaxed rate. Predicting just what may or may not be comfortable at this internal level of feeling isn't always easy or even possible in advance. Thus, getting acquainted with this stepping back routine is a good reparenting practice. Some Adult Children are inclined to overcommit or shut down experiments with themselves in recovery, having no idea what their normal pace might be. Just getting into a habit of learning to use safety nets is a big step in self-care for some of us.

Here's How To!

In the Table 8.1 on the next page familiarize yourself with the elements that comprise an effective Guided Visualization/ Active Imagination.

Next, read the Stage I Guided Visualization included below. Note how each of the elements is handled. You may substitute other pictures for the ones we have used, but be sure you keep in *all* the elements, because, omitting any of these in Stage I, may leave the process incomplete or ineffective for you.

Centering

Relaxation

Begin by taking in some deep, deep relaxing breaths of sparkling fresh air. Allow your breathing to become rhythmic as it slows and becomes deeper and more peaceful. Feel the air, fresh sweet air that sparkles with the silvery-golden light filling it. Feel it as it flows smoothly and deeply into your lungs. Allow your lungs to carry this silvery-golden light into your pulsing, flowing bloodstream. This light will spread healing and relaxation throughout your entire body. If there is anywhere in any organ of your body where you are experiencing tension or any feeling of discomfort, direct this flow of

Table 8.1. Elements of an Effective Guided Visualization/Active Imagination

Stage I

Centering
Relaxing
Grounding
Protecting
Anchoring

Sanctuary
Entering
Expanding visual/feeling
Returning
Anchoring

Exploring
Setting up personal VCR
Scanning
Freeze framing/
other features

Altering History
Rewriting script
Hiring/firing

Transition

Rescuing/Empowering
Joining Inner Child
Summoning allies
Supporting Inner Child

Stage II
(Back to Normal Consciousness)

Reconnecting
Entering picture
Using all senses
Allowing feelings to
surface

Stepping Back to Sanctuary
Pausing
Remembering
Coming/going

healing light to that place now. If you wish, you can move this soft silvery-golden light around like a sparkler of healing, releasing tensions or discomforts in any organ or part of your own body. You may wish to notice especially your neck, your shoulders or anywhere that little knots of tension may accumulate.

Grounding

Imagine that you have flexible metallic cords of pure earth energy extending from the bottoms of your feet into the very molten core and center of the planet Earth. These cords in no way restrict your movements; instead they create a constant flowing pulse or powerful, glittery and bright energy that circulates into your body. This energy from the center of the planet is magnetic; if you choose to do so, you can let it magnetically attract any toxins or any toxic-feeling memories from anywhere within your body or mind, and take them back into the deep powerful molten center of the planet Earth. The pressure in the Earth's core is very great and powerful so that it takes all of those toxins and impurities and turns them into jewels. This pressure turns these carbons, these experiences of painful thoughts into beautiful sparkling diamonds, sapphires, rubies and other riches. These treasures are yours to keep and use for adornment or to exchange for the nourishments you need.

Protecting

Now expand the light that fills you, mixing the fresh sweet air that you breathe into your lungs and bloodstream with the magnetic richness of the Earth's energy. You can surround yourself completely with radiant glittery blue-golden light. This light protects you totally. All that enters is for your highest good and healing. Anything that is not important for your healing and enjoyment is no longer drawn to you but is sent harmlessly away. You are entirely in charge of your own process. You direct it and move easily, experiencing your connectedness and safety through your grounding cords and as you breathe in deeply and relax. Pause now, for a minute, and feel the power of your connectedness and safety within this fountain of glittery blue-golden light. Experience it flowing over you from the very center of your crown as a cascading fountain of healing and protecting light that you direct and move just as you wish. Take a deep breath and allow yourself to experience this power and protection.

Anchoring

Every time you choose to experience this sense of feeling powerfully centered, just take a deep relaxing breath. These cords of metallic energy connecting you to the powerful energy within the Earth are yours to keep. They are joined together with the light that fills your lungs with air and with every breath you take. This process of self-healing becomes more and more a natural and integrated aspect of your Inner Being. Every time you consciously undertake this process by taking a minute to breathe in a deep, refreshing breath, it becomes easier and easier with each repetition to experience and to direct this healing to yourself, or to the others in your life with whom you are connected in your heart.

Sanctuary

Entering

As you continue to experience this healing and protection, imagine yourself entering *your favorite place.* While keeping your grounding cords connected, breathing deeply and relaxing, imagine you are entering your favorite place. This place is always safe, cheerful, peaceful and beautiful. It can be a place that you remember or a place that you make up. Looking around your favorite place, notice what you see or hear.

Expanding

Once in this place look around and know that it is your own. Perhaps there may be *smells* that bring you feelings of happiness or safety. Add or move around whatever you'd like to arrange another way. In this place, you are safe, you are in

control and nothing and no one interferes. This is your place
of healing.

Returning

You can return to this favorite place anytime you choose.
You have a beautiful golden key that belongs to you alone. No
one enters here but you. You can have peacefulness here at
any moment of the night or day, without fear of this safe,
protected place vanishing or being violated. You have the
only golden key to this sanctuary of your Inner Life.

Anchoring

You may wish to locate a place in your own body and to
touch the place right now. Whenever you choose to return to
your favorite place, you can do so instantly, just by touching
that special place on your body and taking a deep breath. All
of what you have experienced here returns and enables you
to easily reconnect yourself to this process of healing that you
have now created. If you choose, you can touch this special
place on your body while you are listening to music and bring
the music with you to this Sanctuary. (If this is a prelude to
Stage II, continue with the Stage II processes. If not, then
complete the following experience to return to normal
waking consciousness.)

Transition

Return to full and alert consciousness at the count from 1 to
3: (1) Look around your Sanctuary; experience the safety and
security you have. Let it fill your heart and flow all through
your body. (2) Feel the tingle of sensations returning to your
body as you move into a waking state of poised and centered
consciousness; feel yourself reentering the present. (3) Now
fully awake, filled with vitality and rested as though you had
taken a wonderful healing nap, you are back and ready to face
your day with a smile. You are alert and alive!

If you are working with a partner, ask him to read you this
Guided Visualization. Or if you are on your own, tape record

the process. Use a gentle but fully audible voice. In the Sanctuary section, be sure to allow enough time between your suggestions so that there is room for your imagination to act without being rushed.

Some people will find it is easier to move on a feeling rather than a visual level. They will *sense* protection or feel the grounding cords. Others *hear* more than *see,* so that the sounds of birds singing, bells tinkling, water rushing or surf crashing against the shore may bring about the peacefulness and security needed to begin self-healing. You may want to adapt the process further by adding meditation or audio tapes.

The return to normal waking consciousness will usually take 15 to 30 minutes. There are no fixed rules of how much time to spend in the process, once you have become used to coming and going and have created an internal sense of Sanctuary. Some people will allow most of the process of self-healing to go on below the conscious level, perhaps spending little time — a minute or two or five, in the midst of their busy schedule. Others will find *going within* a practice that gives real enjoyment, and these persons may *take* the time, perhaps rearranging their schedules. Use Stage I of this Tool as freely as you like. It is made up of "pure healing".

When you are ready, you can begin to utilize Stage II of this process; the basics are sketched here. We invite you to go at a pace comfortable to you while you experiment with mastering this Tool. It is a good idea to interact with others, either by working together, supporting each other's exploration of Inner Space, or by sharing your experiences and insights in discussion. Strange as it may seem at first glance, this Tool, designed to take us within ourselves, turns out to be a major aid for ". . . risking coming out of isolation . . .".

Any of the Stage II elements can be accessed individually (once you have become familiar with the techniques) and combined as you feel appropriate. Remember to follow your *feelings* at all times, whether it means backing off for a little rest and relaxation in your Sanctuary or means trying something new and daring in the process for yourself.

Another point to remember is to always *offer, suggest* and *support* your Inner Child (or other Inner Personalities) rather than ordering or questioning. Finally, avoid asking questions that engage the intellect, such as "What do you *think* about . . .?"

Feelings are the golden cords that reach us from within and guide us in this process. Thinking about these experiences is perfectly okay before and after the process, and can be extremely rewarding and creative. In fact, many find that whole new categories of thought become available to them as the result of these internal journeys.

Now, from within the Stage I Sanctuary, suggest to yourself that you take a walk deeper into Inner Space, perhaps taking a stairway or downward path that takes you *where you need to go* to find out useful and important aspects about yourself. You may find it helpful to make a countdown, going backward from 10 to 1, as you descend the steps or pathway. Suggesting that your body feels lighter is often helpful, too. Take a few minutes to do this transition. When you have become comfortably settled in the privacy of your own Inner Being, you are ready to begin exploring.

Exploring

Notice the physical place you've entered. No matter where you are — castle, beach, forest, etc. — you will notice a comfortable place to sit with a VCR monitor/remote control. This is your personal VCR. You have dozens and dozens of your own tapes that you can drop in and view. If you are in touch with your Inner Child, she or he can join you on the couch as you scan your tapes. (Let the Child decide which one to view.) Your remote control gives you complete control. You can stop the action, replay, adjust the volume, go to slow motion or whatever seems appropriate so that you and your Inner Child are safe and secure from danger. If the memories are especially painful or frightening, you can distance yourself still another level by putting you and your Child on the moon, where you can see yourselves back there on the couch watching the film.

Reconnecting

You may choose to enter any scene or picture that appears. You can *become* your Inner Child, seeing/speaking from the *present tense* and reliving this experience again. Feel, hear and smell the situation. Allow your feelings to become the feelings of your Inner Child. If this upsets or frightens you, take some deep breaths and experience your Sanctuary again, while remaining in the picture with your Child. Try to let these feelings emerge freely. It's okay to cry. It's okay to be angry. Nothing you do in your Inner Child can harm or damage anyone, however violent or bitter these old feelings may be. You experience them as part of your own healing.

Rescuing

To get in touch with your Adult Self, let your Adult Self enter this scene and pick up, hug or touch your Inner Child. Tell your Inner Child that you will be there, will protect, will take home with you or will stand up for your Child. Do whatever your Adult Self feels or your Child asks to make the scene safe for your Child. This can still include "freeze framing" (as done with a VCR remote control) a parent figure so that the Child can get out his feelings *safely*. If your Adult Self feels inclined to have some extra help, take anyone you wish into the scene. This can mean bringing: (1) Superman to stand up to Daddy for you, (2) a number of people who have been lied to, to hear the truth, or (3) the God of your understanding to radiate love and power in a situation where there had been none.

Altering History

Realize that you and your Inner Child are entirely free to alter this experience. After all, you have an absolute right to peace, tranquility and joyousness within your Inner World. You can hire new Inner Parents, *perfect ones* who give your Inner Child (and each other) exactly what is needed and who unconditionally love and appreciate your Child Within. Even if the old parents are reluctant to move out, you can either force them to do so or to reform themselves. If the latter, ask them directly, "Are you here within my Inner Sanctuary for my highest good?" They will *have to go* or *change* unless they can answer with an unqualified, "Yes, I am!" You have a perfect right to unconditional loyalty, love and support from *all* your Inner Personalities. You deserve unqualified love and it's definitely there for you in your Sanctuary.

Using means that comes to mind, you can change or modify any scene or interaction. This includes using your VCR remote control to do whatever seems appropriate, such as replaying scenes so that your Inner Child is *heard* and *heeded.* It's also possible to use spiritual power to heal or rectify what may be impossible to overcome directly. If that seems okay to you, you can go back to previous lives and reconnect with powerful Inner Guides to channel wisdom. You may wish to locate your own Inner Mate, as well, if you long for a sense of heartfelt companionship as a constant in your life.

One man, *Ray G.,* once made the comment that, if you find yourself in a memory situation that overwhelms you, go back to a lifetime when you were a Perfect Master to experience renewal and insight for your own personal answer. As you become more at home within, *experiment.*

Remember, in Active Imagination processes, your imagination is in charge and has only the limits of what you decide is personally acceptable as restraints. Because no action is taken outside of your own mind, there need be no holding back or repression of feelings, fantasies or wishes. Active Imagination deals only with the content of our own "mental worlds", where each of us has a complete right to peace, support and freedom. Any action we may take in settling old scores; getting unruly parents, siblings or lovers to behave; or clearing up communications for our Inner Child's security or self-esteem operates internally within our minds exclusively. This internal action never includes acting on others in physical reality. Anything goes and no one need concern himself about external standards of acceptability. In Active Imagination, each of us is free to be our own standard of acceptability.

Stepping Back To Sanctuary

Anytime you find yourself becoming scattered, separated or panicky in any of these Stage II procedures and experiences, *pause* and take in a few deep, relaxing breaths. Remember that you are in control of your own process here and are safely within your Inner Sanctuary. Feel blue-golden light. Let this fountain of pure healing flood over you and protect you. Reexperience *your favorite place*. Taking all the time you need, experience your safety, power and personal control of your own process. If you like, go back into Stage II or return to full consciousness, using a transition similar to the Guided Visualization example we included at the end of Stage I.

Some people notice an upswing in dream activities soon after they begin utilizing Guided Visualization/Active Imagination practices. If you notice this or would like to increase your dream awareness, give yourself some suggestions while you are in your Sanctuary. For example, perhaps my Inner Guides will bring an answer to these questions in my dreams, and it will be clear and vivid so that I will have no trouble understanding and remembering. If the dreams you are experiencing seem frightening, ask your healing tools (the grounding cords and light) to flood your dream experiences and keep you safe and warm in sleep!

Most people find that these visualizations have a wonderful effect on their entire program for recovery/discovery and add whole new dimensions to the Steps. We suggest you start with Step 11, using Guided Visualization as an aid in your meditations, and allow your Inner Child to guide your process. We'd like to *welcome* you to this new experience of healing. Keep coming back.

Becoming Your Own Loving Parent Exercise

This exercise can be used to work all of the 12 Steps with reparenting as the focus.

Use with Guided Visualization/Active Imagination, Tool II. Imagine you are deciding to become the parent of a needy Child who has great potential and promise.

1. How do you feel about the prospect of this new responsibility?

2. What support do you need, *yourself*, in order to do a really good job for this important Child of yours?

3. Considering your Child now, has your Child suffered from *neglect* that requires attention? For example, (does your Child need a medical checkup or dental work? Does he deserve nicer surroundings or environment so that he can flower? How about educational needs?)

4. What *guidance* and *encouragement* does this Child need? (Is this Child shy or withdrawn in group situations? Does he get frustrated easily and give up or bristle under criticism? How about habits or addictions that really need attention?)

5. What *values* do you already have that you want to share and model for your Child?

6. What are your hopes, as a parent, for this new relationship? (Do you wish for a Child who will cheer your old age with joy [and maybe grandchildren] or a Child who will make a great name for your family? Do you long for trust and love to flow between you, free and constant as the sun?)

7. What activities will you personally commit to, to nurture and build your relationship with your Child? (What about regular, healthful exercise and diet? What sorts of play will you make a priority? Can your Child interrupt you when he needs love? Will you give this Child hugs?) Try to be very clear about these commitments. They will mean a great deal to your Child, and keeping them will do a lot to develop trust between you.

9 ACCEPTING A HIGHER POWER OF OUR UNDERSTANDING

An Exercise In Working Steps 2, 3 or 11.

If you don't have a concept of God (or an understanding of spirituality) you feel you *can* comfortably *accept,* or if you wish to expand the concept of God you do presently have, we suggest some ways you may find to bring these abstract concepts to a closer, more *personal* level for yourself.

Using Tool II, Guided Visualization/Active Imagination, go to your Inner Sanctuary (Stage I) and expand on your feelings of connectedness, trust, safety and healing while in this Inner Space. Allow this place and your personal feelings of serenity to be your Higher Power. Utilize the Tool as your meditation and prayer.

Using Tool II, Stage II, Guided Visualization/Active Imagination, turn on your personal VCR and view a tape in which you create a *loving* God of your understanding. Feel free to keep making changes until you've found a God you feel you can trust. Create a drawing that represents your spiritual self. Meditate on this expression, allowing a sense of joy, wholeness and trust to connect with your conception. For now, allow this drawing to represent your understanding of a

Higher Power, and visualize it hanging on the wall in your personal Sanctuary.

Go to an actual physical place on or nearby your property. Allow your favorite tree, rock or spot on a riverbank to bring you in touch with your present understanding of a Higher Power. If you play an instrument or sing, allow the connection you feel with the music to bring you in touch with your Higher Power. Tune in your own heartbeat; sense, feel and hear your connection with this "universal drum". Or, look into a campfire and experience your personal connection to the universe; imagine you are looking into the heart of a star.

Welcoming Envy, Jealousy And Contempt

Practically *no one* wants to admit to feeling envious or jealous, or to having contempt for those who we like to think have *less* ability than we do. It *may be* okay to be angry, upset, hurt or sad, or to have a good justification for putting someone down; however, it's hard to think of a situation where it feels okay to be frankly envious or jealous, or to hold someone up to ridicule or contempt.

Realistically, many of us do have these sorts of feelings, and often we deny them.

The purpose of this Exercise is to develop a reparenting relationship in which our Inner Child can trust enough to come out of denial and admit to these sorts of "wrong feelings" in perfect safety without fear of punishment or rejection.

For the purposes of this Exercise, our Adult Self agrees to welcome expressions of envy, jealousy or fantasy involving put-downs, rejection, ridicule or contempt of others. The Inner Child is asked to trust and accept this format as a safe place to share these feelings and fantasies, and to accept this offer of reparenting as a part of healing denial and repression that may be seriously in the way for both the Child and the Adult Self.

Here's How To Do It

1. Using the Fourth or Tenth Step Inventory or any other method of getting in touch with your resentments,

notice who and what you resent, hate and fear, or what
makes you shut down completely. Be as specific as
you can be. *Whom* are/were you mad at or afraid of?
What *institutions* do you feel helpless about? What
social or *family* situations seem entirely impossible for
you to handle, accept or change?

2. Ask your Inner Child to respond to the following
   questions, in perfect safety:

   - What does each person, institution or family
     member have that I don't, but very much wish
     I had? (**Envy**)

   - What are they doing and getting away with that
     I feel is unfair or unjust, and that I don't feel
     I personally could do or get away with?
     (**Jealousy**)

   - What things do these persons, institutions or
     social/family situations *act out*, that I am deeply
     afraid may also be true about *me?* (**Contempt**)

3. After each response by the Inner Child, welcome the
   shared admission of envy, jealousy or contempt,
   saying such words as, "Your trust is safe with me, Little
   Child. I welcome and appreciate your trust."

4. Supporting your Inner Child, look over the Victim
   Wheel (Tool I) and notice how each denied feeling
   has limited both the Child and the Adult Self's
   perspective. From the Freedom Wheel notice what
   affirmations are involved. Affirm that your Child and
   your Adult have access to whatever good the blocked
   feelings prevented. For example, if your Child was

envious of someone who had more power on the job,
affirm to your Child and your Adult that you *also can*
have power, and that no one can prevent you from
developing your own power as a living reality. For
yourself, affirm that you can have (and have a perfect
right to enjoy) any good you perceive in anyone else,
and that no injustice can prevent your healing or block
the good in your own life.

5. Using the Guided Visualization/Active Imagination
   Tool II, allow your Inner Child to act out the fantasy
   put-downs or ridicule actions. Permit your Adult Self to
   support and encourage your Child to do this while
   releasing pent up anger and denied feelings of pain, as
   freer feelings begin to take root. Notice any feelings
   you experience of greater self-trust and self-acceptance
   as you experiment with this process.

Intimacy Inventory: Step 4

Part I: Models

1. What was your earliest concept of intimacy?

2. Scan the period when you were a teenager, beginning
   with puberty, to get an idea of the role models you
   had at that time. This is an excellent subject for Stage
   II, Active Imagination.

3. Looking at this time in your life as a time when you
   were forming your concepts of intimacy, ask yourself:

   • What books influenced you?

   • Who were the adult role models and what were

their relationships? How did you feel then about these *role models* and their relationships?

• What television shows did you watch?

• What music and lyrics did you most enjoy?

• What seemed most important to you during your early teen years?

• What were your ideas or fantasies about the partner you desired?

• How did you communicate your feelings in these early relationships?

• If you didn't communicate your feelings, what did you do instead?

• What types or styles of people attracted you?

• How did you dress?

- How did they dress?

- What values or behaviors made another person
  attractive to you?

4. Check out your ideas of intimacy today. How much are
   these current ideas the same as your early ones?

5. Revise your concept of intimacy now, based on
   everything you've learned and observed, including
   your revised hopes for yourself in recovery.

Part II: Creating The Perfect Relationship

Now, let's imagine that you have complete freedom to
create, in an unlimited way, your perfect intimate relationship.
Get comfortable. Go to your favorite place, using Guided
Visualization/Active Imagination. Begin to imagine this de-
lightful intimate relationship. Be ready to write your images or
feelings about it, or to speak into a tape recorder. *Create*
without trying to make it rational. Pretend that you can have
what you wish very easily, no matter what. It doesn't have to
make sense. This is your creation; keep changing it until you
like it.

Pay attention to your feelings. What words are spoken (if
any) and in what tone of voice? What senses of smell, taste
and touch do you experience? Where are you? Are you
somewhere in the world, a place you remember, or is it a
totally unfamiliar place? Notice everything. Get as much
information as possible.

When you get your creation just the way you want it for the
present (knowing you can, at any time, go back in the Guided
Visualization and change it), ask yourself such questions as,
"Is this the intimacy I want?" "How do I feel, feeling this

intimacy?" (Imagine you do have it — experience the emotions, thoughts and sensations.) "In order to have this kind of life relationship: (1) what will I have to add to my current belief system about intimate relationships and (2) what thoughts or beliefs that I currently have may have to be replaced about intimate relationships?"

Part III: Being Intimate With Myself

Based on Part II, ask yourself:

1. Am I willing to develop this idea of an intimate relationship with myself?

2. How intimate am I, at present, with myself?

3. In what ways can I give the quality of nurturing, support, care and tenderness to myself that I desire from others?

4. Am I really willing to be there for myself?

Part IV: Being Intimate With Your Inner Mate

Using Guided Visualization/Active Imagination, Stage II, ask your Inner Mate to join you now, and ask her or him the questions from Part III of this inventory.

Developing an Inner Mate who loves and cares for both your Adult Self and your Inner Child is a valuable resource for self-unification. Emotionally, this Inner Mate can be your lover within, the contrasexual other who is always available to you with unconditional love and loyalty. Developing this inner personality gives each of us an expression to fully balance our human potential, letting the other side of our nature express itself in a natural, supportive and unifying manner.

J's Sharing Of The Intimacy Inventory: Step 5

"My experience has been that all my intimate relationships in the past were a direct reflection (a mirror) of my ability and willingness to be intimate with myself. And before my recovery began, my relationship with myself was far from what today I would call intimate.

"As I scanned my past experience of intimacy. I noticed that the relationships I considered intimate were exclusively those that were sexual. Yet, as I look back, I realize that my sexual relationships seemed to lack the sense of caring, nurturing and honesty that my nonsexual friendships seemed able to reach (at times, anyway).

"I considered myself a very open, warm, affectionate and loving person who was very comfortable with my sexuality. This may have been true; but in hindsight, I've also admitted that sex could actually be a way for me to avoid any intimacy other than physical.

"For me, it was less threatening to make love with my partner than it was to address any issue that may have been present in our relationship, or to honestly express my feelings or to get in touch with my own needs or views. Sex could be a way to elude any close examination of myself or of our interactions.

As I have become increasingly willing to be intimate with myself in recovery, I've increasingly experienced a growing sense of personal security and greater freedom to taking sharing risks in the important relationships in my life. I feel more satisfied in my personal relationship with myself and with others. Also, in my partnership, my sexual relating seems more truly a dance instead of an avoidance."

Mixed Feelings Exercises

Feeling More Than One Feeling

It isn't unusual to have *more than one feeling* toward an activity or an individual, especially when something important and close to the heart is involved. For example, we've all experienced being angry or disappointed at the behavior of those we love from time to time. Most of us have experienced anxiety or fear associated with activities we really want to *do well,* such as taking tests, succeeding at job interviews, communicating with family members or sweethearts, playing or making love. Often we are inclined to make internal judgments as to which feelings are right and which are wrong for a situation or relationship. These judgments lead us to *deny, stuff* or *counterfeit* our feelings even with ourselves.

In this exercise, "scan" yourself using Guided Visualization/Active Imagination, Stage II (the VCR screen) and notice any relationships or situations in your life that tend to create these sorts of conflicts for you.

If these are Adult Child issues, consider Steps 1, 2 and 3:

1. Are you powerless over yourself in some internal conflict situations?

2. Do you say or do things which are dishonest, and therefore, need to be guided back to the sanity of honesty and integrity?

3. Are you willing to accept your Higher Power's guidance and to stop judging yourself?

Feeling And Coloring

Using the circle provided in Figure 9.1, color your *feelings.* Work from the edges of the circle, which represent your "self", toward the center, which represents your "heart". This is a good exercise to do while talking to a trusted friend or sponsor. Use as many colors as you wish and make them as

Figure 9.1. "Color Your Feelings" Circle

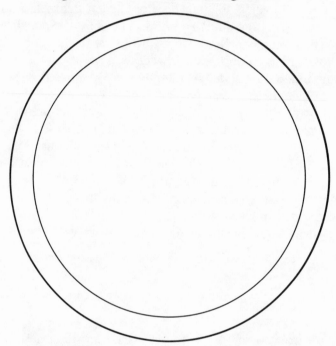

dark or light as feels appropriate. Try sticking with *shapes* and *areas* of color instead of drawing specific objects in this exercise. Date and put your "circle" up where you can appreciate it for a week or so (with or without a title). This is a creative way to explore Step 4. If you do this while talking about your feelings to a trusted friend, therapist or sponsor, it is also part of doing Step 5. At this stage of the process you *need not* tell any persons involved toward whom your feelings are centered. How you eventually deal with relating to others will be determined later in Steps 8 and 9. Honesty of feelings isn't necessarily bound to "being an open book", or to "wearing one's heart on the sleeve". Remember to allow Steps 6 and 7 to influence your personal development.

Feelings And Creative Writing

Probably most good literature in the world has been produced by people who feel *strongly* or who have often experienced conflict, anxiety or sadness mixed with tenderness, desire or hopes for love and fellowship. Mixed feelings can be a source of creative power, once we are willing to acknowledge them.

A good way to acknowledge these feeling levels without risking open conflict or unpredictable results in our daily lives is to use them as materials for writing poetry, plays, short stories or whatever appeals. Taking a class or joining a writers' workshop is a good way to have an opportunity to share these feelings with people and in an appropriate setting. The fear many of us have of being challenged about the truth or fantasy of whatever is felt and expressed is reduced by using a creative writing outlet. It is perfectly acceptable for the imagination to run entirely free using this outlet.

Two example poems containing different sorts of mixed feelings follow:

Sunday Morning

We went out and gathered herbs
and dug the garlic bulging and alive
to dry
I leaned my body on your shoulder
from behind and met your eyes
once with my face
and tangled wind opened tangled grass
my inward stillness was a spike
a dragon's fire stabbing through
  my body of loose bones
and flesh too soft to keep a shape
the morning with brown baskets
brimming and sunlight's fragrance close
your hands were slight quick-moving
graces that eluded meaning
and I leaned across your chest
to let the dragons leap across
your bones
protest at the solitude of living

Raven
(April, 1972)

Wandering

Rarely ever do I see a snake — I saw one
today — I couldn't say for sure
if it were a rattlesnake or not — having
no rattles — but that is common
for a youngish smallish snake as this one
was — he appeared to have
pits behind his eyes — his head
was large and flat compared
to the rest of him and he
may have had diamonds on his back — I
tickled him with a twig where he was
stretched out across the old sand road — he
didn't coil but just stuck out his tongue and
slithered quietly away
smooth-moving creatures snakes
my neighbors often see them — kill them — usually
with guns — but I don't
often see them although I've
lived here years and years
and live here more than anyone — I
wouldn't want to tread on one —
especially a neighbor with a gun or
pits behind his eyes or not recognize
a viper out of context — why
I wonder do I see them rarely
when the world's convinced they are an everpresent
danger? I must live a life in parallel
to everybody else and not
quite touch the realm of snakes
except for curiosity
extending twigs and tongues or
should I be
afraid?

Raven
(June 14, 1983)

Agree/Disagree Meditation Exercise On Feeling Feelings

In this exercise, let yourself feel whatever emerges from you as you read the quotations and notice whether or not what the author has shared communicates to you, *on a feeling level.* Does the image take you to a place inside that *feels* honest? Or do the words seem hollow to you? Imagine that you are the writer's audience and critic, that you've gone back in time to visit and that the authors are very interested in your response to this comment shared here. What do you have to say to them?

> *If* [someone] *suddenly sees a child about to fall into a well, they will all without exception experience a feeling of alarm and distress. They will feel so, not as a ground on which they may gain favor of the child's parents, nor as a ground on which they may seek the praise of their neighbors and friends, nor from a dislike of the reputation of having been unmoved by such a thing.*
>
> Mencius, Chinese (372-289 BC)

> *We think so because other people think so;*
> *Or because — or because — after all, we do think so;*
> *Or because we were told so, and think we must think so*
> *Or because we once thought so, and think we still think so;*
> *Or because having thought so, we think we will think so.*
>
> Henry Sidgwick, English (1838-1900)

> *Govern a great enterprise as you would fry a small fish.*
>
> Lao-Tzu, Chinese (604-531 BC)

It is when we try to grapple with another [person's] *intimate need that we perceive how incomprehensible, wavering and misty are the beings that share with us the sight of the stars and the warmth of the sun.*

Joseph Conrad, Polish (1857-1924)

All [her] *his faults were such that one loves* [her] *him still the better for them.*

Oliver Goldsmith, English (1728-1774)

. . . I was drifting sand in the wind of the world's anger.
It is just fate that has brought me back alive.
The fence gate is filled with neighbors' faces,
Sighting and shedding a few tears.
In the deep night we light a new candle
And see each other face to face as in a dream.

Tu Fu, Chinese (712-770)

The old Quaker was right: "I expect to pass through this life but once. If there is any kindness, or any good thing I can do to my fellow beings, let me do it now. I shall pass this way but once."

William Gannett, American (1840-1924)

Do not ask from people what Nature has denied them . . . Do not beg the monkey to have fine deportment, nor the ox nor the donkey to have a sweet voice.

Iacopone Da Todi, Italian (died 1306)

The wish to be independent of all [others] *and not to be under obligation to any one is the sure sign of a soul without tenderness.*

Joseph Joubert, French (1754-1824)

*There was, however, one small incident of my
boyhood days which . . . must have meant a good
deal to me or it would not have stayed in my
memory, clear and sharp, vivid and shadowless, all
these slow-drifting years. We had a little slave boy
whom we had hired from someone, there in
Hannibal. He was from the eastern shore of
Maryland, and had been brought away from his
family and friends, halfway across the American
continent and sold. He was a cheery spirit,
innocent and gentle, and the noisiest creature that
ever was, perhaps. All day long he was singing,
whistling, yelling, whooping, laughing — it was
maddening, devastating, unendurable. At last, one
day, I lost all my temper, and went raging to my
mother and said Sandy had been singing for an
hour without a single break, and I couldn't stand it,
and* wouldn't *she please shut him up. The tears
came into her eyes and her lip trembled, and she
said something like this:*

*"Poor thing, when he sings it shows that he is not
remembering, and that comforts me; but when he
is still I am afraid he is thinking and I cannot bear
it. He will never see his mother again; if he can sing,
I must not hinder it, but be thankful for it. If you
were older, you would understand me; then that
friendless child's noise would make you glad."*

Mark Twain, American (1835-1910)

Do you find it hard to identify within yourself some of the
feelings expressed in these quotations? Do some of the
quotations elicit feelings you have difficulty naming?

Imagine these authors as sponsors or parent figures and
practice expressing your feelings (whatever they may be) to
them in a meditation utilizing Guided Visualization/Active
Imagination. Allow them to speak back to you in response.
Look at any memories that these quotations prompt and note
them (or *draw* them) when you finish your meditation.

Feelings Exercises To Use With Physical Exercise

Sometimes when a person with a dysfunctional childhood history starts an exercise program to get physically fit, powerful *feelings* begin to surface. These feelings seem to be subtlely associated with physical play, sports activities or just feeling good physically! Feeling associations of disappointment and loneliness, or painful memories of being attacked, ridiculed or rejected are among the most common play-bonded physical memories experienced by Adult Children.

When such associations of negative feeling are bonded to play and exercise oriented activities, many find they've developed lifestyles (and bodies) that are sedentary or mental.

They may take the role of spectator in life not only regarding sports and games. For example, sexual relating can be much affected, characterized by passivity or anxiety, which interferes with the expression of tenderness or passion. This may occur even though overt sexual issues or misconduct were not present in the childhood home. In terms of physical expression, feelings may not be repressed but remain blocked.

In addition, associations of pain or sadness with self-assertion stemming from play memories may influence nonassertive behavior in work-related or other social situations. Self-esteem may be affected, often with no *conscious awareness* because we *avoid* the physical activities subconsciously associated with childhood loss, rejection or ridicule. We're "too busy" or "don't care for" those sorts of activities.

It often takes a weight or health issue to motivate us to relating to ourselves as *physical human beings* again. For one reason or another, we decide to get in shape, only to find ourselves flooded with memories or feeling associations that make it seem impossible to continue, even though the exercise routine may not be very physically taxing. Our excuses of being too busy or not liking it make it possible for us to return to our old ruts. These ruts are actually dysfunctional traps. If we allow ourselves to revert to them, we may be secure from buried feeling associations, but at a potential great cost to our bodies in terms of health, premature aging or reduced enjoyment.

These exercises-with-exercises are designed to break up these ruts, using techniques of Visualization with physical exercise. If you aren't troubled by difficult feeling associations with exercise, these routines can be used anyway to add some new dimensions to any simple workout.

Welcoming And Affirming Feelings

1. Take a few minutes to center yourself using Guided Visualization.
2. Begin your exercise program while recalling your buried *feelings,* memories and old associations. Speaking directly to your Inner Child, *invite* your Child to share these buried experiences with you now.
3. Continue your exercise routine, letting your feelings arise. If it is at all possible, arrange to do your exercise routine somewhere where it is safe to cry, shout, scream or talk aloud. Use about half your allotted exercise period to *open up* to these memories, feelings and your personal associations with past events.
4. While continuing to move through your exercise routine, return your awareness to your personal Sanctuary and surround yourself with glowing, silvery-golden light, flood yourself with vital earth-centered energies and allow the magnetic flow of these energies to move through *your entire body,* carrying the painful, poisonous feelings and memories back into the center of the receptive, healing Earth.
5. Speak (or shout) *positive statements* (affirmations) directly *at* the voices, memory images or feelings that you are experiencing and releasing, while continuing to visualize your Stage I healing light. "I love myself enough to give myself good health," "God doesn't make junk!" or any short and to-the-point affirmation is good. Doing this tends both actively to erase old tapes and to replace them with positive, life-embracing associations for the present and the future.

Exploring Physical Symptoms

1. Take a few minutes to center yourself using Guided Visualization.
2. Invite your Inner Child to share your unburied feelings, memories and old associations.
3. Notice any areas or places in your body where pain, discomfort, nausea, cramps or other physical symptoms are located. Using Guided Visualization/Active Imagination, advise your Inner Child to *enter that place,* becoming small enough to do so, perhaps by riding into the affected area by canoe in your bloodstream? (Why not? Be creative.) Do this while continuing the exercise routine and experiencing the symptom, whatever it may be. Ask your Inner Child to look around the affected place in your body and to run any film clips she may find there for you on your personal VCR.
4. While looking at the VCR, let any feelings surface and continue the exercise. Notice any pain, discomfort or humiliation your Inner Child is experiencing in the film clips. Speak directly to your Inner Child, offering your support, rescue or approval to your Child, as feels appropriate. Encourage your Inner Child to ask you directly for whatever she or he needs or wants in the situation. You are free to use any means you wish to give this Child the unconditional love and support required to heal this incident or feeling. (Be creative.) If your Inner Child wants to act out in anger over this old situation, support her in doing this, because this releases pent up feelings that have been blocked or trapped in your body. Surround the Child and yourself in clear golden, silvery or electric blue light, and finish the exercise program as you bond with your Inner Child.

Updating And Revising Play Experiences

1. Center yourself using Guided Visualization.
2. Share your unburied feelings, memories and old associations with your Inner Child.

3. Utilizing Guided Visualization/Active Imagination, ask your Inner Child to *take charge* of your imagination and to create any play or sports experiences she would have liked or enjoyed in the past. Do these imagination experiences as here-and-now visualizations. If, for example, your Child liked to be swung around and tossed in the air, visualize yourself sharing that experience with your Inner Child *right now,* while continuing your exercise routine. Give your Inner Child permission to fully experience the joy and well-being she associates with this play activity visualization. Also give yourself permission to experience these feelings as you bond and experience through the Child.

4. While continuing to experience through the Child's feelings and continuing your exercise routine, express to the Child your willingness for her to have joyful, healthy experiences in physical play and all activities of her body. Encourage and praise your Inner Child. Surround your Child and yourself with a flowing rainbow of multicolored light that extends into the center of the earth. Invite your Child to select any colors she chooses to heal and strengthen the heart, body or mind, and to feel love and health as a birthright in a Spiritual Universe. Experience this feeling of bonding and nourishing while you complete your exercise routine.

Expanding New Choices

1. Using Guided Visualization center yourself.
2. Share your unburied feelings, memories and old associations with your Inner Child.
3. After clearing out the painful memories and consciously replacing those old associations with pleasurable and satisfying ones (using the previous three Exercises), join with your Inner Child and explore the freedom you have made available to yourself. *Feel it:* any more fear, pain or guilt while being physically

active? If not, you are free to explore and expand while going through your exercise routine. Sing. Recite poetry. Think about math, physics or computer logic. Solve problems. With your mind, emotions and body unified and at peace, focus your attention on *whatever you wish.* You are *free.* If you are no longer haunted by feelings and old conflicts that had been anchored to your experience of yourself as a physical being, then you will probably find it enjoyable to explore your thinking and your feeling selves, with less fear of risk. Acknowledge this achievement. Expand on it for yourself. Thank yourself. Give yourself a big gold star. **You deserve it!**

These exercises-with-exercise work most easily with simple activities such as walking, running, bicycling, jumping rope or rowing. If you choose to use them with more complicated workouts or dance routines, select ones you are familiar with or are not too challenged by, so that you won't be trying to learn both the exercise routine and this emotional-clearing process at the same time. These exercises-with-exercise will work best with four to five repetitions per week for at least a four- to six-week commitment. After four to six weeks, expect to be on friendlier, healthier terms with your body and your Inner Child.

10 TOOL III: CREATIVE ACTION ROUTINES

In recovery, taking action is a testimony to progress. Seeing ourselves and our experiences alter for the better, finding ourselves able to succeed in terms of our own values and feeling ourselves truly free of limitations that had kept us back from life are the rewards of our willingness to becoming our own loving parents.

Taking action is about *willingness.* Beginning with the first steps out of *denial,* willingness is motivation and remains a reliable "reality check". This reality check asks, "Are we willing to act on new information, to let the new behavior replace the old and to accept ourselves as healthy and whole human beings?"

In terms of the 12 Steps, willingness to change is the core of Step 6 where we ask ourselves, "What no longer serves me? Am I willing to let it go, to make a real change in how I live, one day at a time?"

Willingness is an inner readiness that comes before change; it is an enthusiastic, hopeful feeling. Adult Children may have this desire and enthusiasm to change inside, but often feel stifled or clumsy when it comes to actually taking the risk to reaching out (or to be seen).

On feeling levels the concept "we *are* what we *do*" is a key and affects self-concept in subtle but pervasive ways. If, for example, we were abused or intimidated children in dysfunctional families, we probably learned to survive by cringing, rebelling, lying or sneaking; it is likely that we internalized self-loathing and shame toward ourselves, in addition to learning some self-defeating behaviors.

We gain insight as we come out of denial. Lasting recovery becomes a reality as we are able to risk acting on this new information and to internalize a new feeling experience of who we really are. We are able to stand tall, negotiate, speak and act out of integrity. We develop effective new behaviors and also gain the great blessing that comes from feeling ourselves free of behaviors which we, ourselves, rejected all along.

Inner shame we had internalized as victims in alcoholic or dysfunctional homes, is released by action. These actions are our own and we can respect them. Step 9 of the 12 Steps operates to release *us* as we are able to act from our hearts.

The Creative Action Routines in Tool III are a collection of dramatic techniques designed to provide structure and support for bringing concepts, feelings and behaviors into the reality of experience. These routines create a context in which it is safe to take risks. For Adult Children, this is especially important. As we become able to take these risks, we experience overcoming our fears of being ridiculed, being victimized, self-negating, appearing silly or stupid, appearing better than or less than others, or **not being perfect**.

Our previous concepts and behavior patterns remain embedded in our physical bodies, imprinted by our past physical experiences. Some Adult Children may be more or less unaware of their bodies as a result of these experiences and *unable to feel,* physically or emotionally.

Through the routines in Tool III, we allow more nurturing concepts to replace parts of our actual experience in a safe setting. Examples are the concepts of "Don't talk", "Don't trust" or "Don't feel" from Claudia Black's *It Will Never Happen To Me* (1983). Many Adult Children internalized these messages and they became our survival mechanisms. We have memories, both physically and mentally, which prove why these are true statements (or were), based on past (childhood) experience.

From the point of view of recovery, how many memories and physical experiences do we have that give us a physical experience of the opposite messages, "It's okay to talk", "It's okay to trust" or "It's okay to feel"? If we were to take a true/ false quiz that had these statements on it, we might answer that these are true statements today. We may *intellectually* believe these statements are true, and we may support *others* in actually doing them. But when it comes time in our own lives to talk, trust and feel, **can we do it?**

Creative Action Routines provide a structured way to create opportunity and a safe place to let some new concepts integrate into experience. As we experience ourselves behaving differently, expressing feelings long-denied or repressed or releasing grief, recovery concepts cease to be mere abstractions. We begin to believe in ourselves and to own our identities as Adult Children in recovery, no longer prisoners of a painful past.

For Adult Children, these Creative Action Routines may seem like the hardest part of recovery, because loss of control is an aspect of letting the healing occur on personal levels as a part of the risk involved in real change. Change *is* risky. Being honest *is* risky. Living free of old ruts *is* risky.

Reparenting ourselves in recovery involves giving ourselves the structure and the support we need to take these risks and to meet life on life's terms. Creative Action can help to develop the habits of courage and self-acceptance that Step 12 implies are necessary to . . . "carry the message . . . and to practice these principles in all our affairs."

Developing A Creative Action Routine

Outline For Structured Play

Concept

Get in touch (memory or imagination) with the behavior or experience to be represented.

- If it is a past experience, decide if you want to play it as it actually was or want to change the outcome.
- If it is a future event you are anticipating, you may choose to play it with the outcome of your worst fears or with your desired ideal outcome.

Casting

- Decide who is going to be in this scene as "characters".
- What is your relationship to the people in this scene?
- What is their relationship to each other?

Plot

Share the basic structure/action or plot format with the co-participants and make yourself an outline.

- What's the story?
- What's the desired outcome?

Development

- What are the specifics (time of day, location, lights?)
- What props do you need?
- Create dialogue: What do you want the characters to do, say or respond? Are there any *key words* or *phrases* you want said? **Note:** The language is always present tense, as if the scene *is taking place now,* including scenes from the past or future. Play people who have died as if they are alive or still have a voice in the present.
- Block out the action (beginning-middle-end). Where do people stand? Do they enter, leave?

Recording

Decide how you will record the information you learn.

- Use a tape or video recorder.
- Have someone take notes.

Play The Scene

- Pay close attention to emotions, thoughts, memories, body language and sensations as you go.
- You are free to freeze the action at any point in order to record your responses as they are happening.
- Read or review feedback.

Incorporate Feedback

Revise and replay the scene until you feel satisfied with your part. Revise the script to include any of the following:

- New understandings and insights
- Body sensations as signals
- Freeing up action or creativity
- Different dialogue, actions or outcome

Example Process: Working Alone With A Mirror

Concept

Examine a future event, such as anxiety in anticipation of a job interview.

Casting

I will do this scene by myself playing two roles, my projected self and the projected employer.

Plot

I've applied for a job and have been called for an interview. The prospective employer's name is Alex Butler. I have no clues as to what he's actually looking for in this position. I do meet the requirements, at least on paper.

My desired outcome is to become aware of what I experience in this particular set of circumstances, to better understand myself. I'm not sure if I *want* the job or not.

Development

The scene takes place in Alex Butler's office in the morning. A large mirror faces a chair where I will sit and observe my whole body. I wear appropriate business clothes. I will be facing Mr. Butler in my imagination. I will introduce myself, shake hands and sit opposite the employer as he describes the specifications of the job. He will ask me questions about my resume. I will respond. Then I will ask him my questions about the job. He will respond. I will thank him and leave.

Recording

I will tape record myself speaking into the mirror.

Play The Scene

I begin the scene by verbalizing for the recording any body sensations, thoughts or feelings I'm having before I enter the room.
(*Recording:* "I feel scared. My hands are sweating and I'm rubbing them together. My heart is pounding. I feel like running away. I keep holding my breath. He's probably not going to want me.")

I enter, introduce myself and sit down.
(*Recording:* "My appearance as far as attire looks pretty good. I look tense. My legs are crossed very tightly, and the pressure on my knees hurts. My hands are clenched together. My eyes look fearful. My body is slightly turned away in a protective position. I keep looking away toward the floor on the right, then back again. I look like someone who's waiting to be eaten alive!")

I imagine that he is describing the job to me. It is a job that interests me, and I feel I would enjoy it. I feel certain I could do the job well.
(*Recording:* "My body is relaxing, a little less tense now. I've uncrossed my legs. I am letting out a deep breath. I'm looking at Mr. Butler as he speaks.")

He asks me if I have any questions.
(*Recording* . . . "I've forgotten them! I have them written down. Here. I feel afraid to ask questions, like I might be

imposing or offensive. My throat is tight. I feel like coughing or choking.")

I read the questions I've prepared. I listen to his responses, thank him and leave.
(*Recording* . . . "I'm glad that's over! I feel like taking a shower or a hot bath. I don't think I did well. I'm not sure I want the job. I'm hungry.")

I review my recordings and listen to the feedback I am giving myself.

Incorporate Feedback

I notice that I defeat myself before I even start with the thoughts I have before I enter the office. I'm not surprised at how tense I looked. It's interesting to be aware of so many body sensations. I wonder if being hungry is a way I find relief from stressful situations?

I decide to play this scene a few times more in different ways:

- Play it *straight through* and afterwards record my memories, thoughts, sensations, etc.
- Play it through *silently,* watching my body, playing with different body postures and noticing any difference in my emotions, thoughts or body sensations.
- Play it through as I did silently, except this time I keep repeating out loud through the whole scene, "I am a very valuable human being!"
- Play it through as if I'm interviewing *him* as a prospective employer for my valuable skills, which are in high demand.

My goal is to explore alternatives and to experience myself acting freely in this situation.

This example can be restructured as a Role Playing Exercise, with a co-participant playing the part of the employer. When working with others, it's a good plan to *switch roles,* letting your co-participant play your part as you play the part of the employer.

Role Playing is a good way to gain skills in telling the truth and communicating effectively in a variety of situations that may feel threatening or risky. Job interviews, dates or assertive behavior with friends or family members are all good concepts for a script.

Introducing Humor

The sharing of joy and laughter is a universal experience of identification and acceptance, dissolving the facades that tend to separate us from ourselves and each other. The ability to laugh is unique to the human species — a spiritual gift.

Physiologically, laughter stimulates internal organs, increases adrenaline and heart rate (similar to exercise), may release endomorphins (the body's natural pain killer) and has an overall effect of relaxation or stress reduction. Some medical doctors and therapists are recommending laughing 15 minutes per day as part of fitness programs. Studies of shame (self-loathing) have shown that the ability to laugh at oneself produces profound healthy relief and dispels shame. Not only does laughter offer us all these benefits, it's also *fun*!

Adult Children may have learned survival mechanisms that abused humor in dysfunctional families. Some may have learned to function as family or social clowns, using humor to mask true feelings or to deflect violence. Others may have retreated and lost touch with their sense of humor or their ability to play. Humor at the expense of another is very hostile to witness or to experience, and those who have been the object of ridicule may have sad, painful associations to heal.

Of course, we are not suggesting that you use humor to mask your true feelings or to ridicule others. Instead we suggest getting in touch with the gleeful squeal of enjoyment. For example, observe the explosive laughter of a child who: (1) sees an adult making a funny face or (2) opens a package for the first time, engaging in wonderment of all the textures, sounds and movements of tearing wrapping paper. Humor can be learned, restored, explored and expanded. Humor can be *practiced,* as an aspect of reparenting our Inner Child, opening up new opportunities to experience and to share joy.

Each of us has a certain uniqueness to our sense of humor, and this is an aspect of a healthy identity. Restoring our innate ability to have fun, to laugh and to be amused is an essential aspect of recovery.

Techniques Of Humor

All humor includes an element of truth and is funny because of the relationship to what is real in our experience. Using various types of distortion, surprise or comparison are ways humor can be introduced. These techniques can be tried to add humor to Creative Action Routines. Experiment in ways that seem appropriate to you.

Shifts In Perspective

1. Spatial: Alter the dimension of distance or closeness
2. Exaggeration: Make things, people, emotions, actions or issues appear much larger than life
3. Understatement: Make things, people, emotions, etc., appear less important than they really are.

Description

1. Detail: Use careful observation to bring out minute features so that they become prominent
2. Analogy: Point out the ways things are alike, or may be seen as similar
3. Juxtaposition: Place things, types of people or environments side by side to exaggerate their differences
4. Personification: Give voice or other human qualities to inanimate objects or animals

Mannerisms

1. Tone of voice: Reveal or conceal emotions.
2. Pacing, rhythm: Measure time, rate of speed in speech and movements.
3. Volume: Sense loudness, softness or silence.

4. Mimicry: Imitate expression, voice, body language, etc.

Surprise

1. Change direction.
2. Shift character.
3. Make sudden movement or stops.
4. Improvise actions or dialogue.

Adding Humor Techniques To Creative Action Routines

Concept

Choose any concept you like.

Casting

Introduce personification or exaggeration to your cast. For example, you may wish to introduce an extraterrestrial who has never witnessed human interaction before.

Plot

Make the plot an extreme case of your worst fears or fondest wishes. Exaggerate or minimize. Do the same thing with the outcome.

Development

Make the whole scene happen in the dark; if embarrassment is an issue, wear a bag over your head and whisper. Do the whole interaction with your back to the person. Perhaps you want to stay in another room and just *yell* dialogue.

If you want to communicate with someone you feel never hears you, have the "actor" play that person with his hands over his ears the whole time while you try different ways to get him to listen or hear.

You may want to have all the characters mimic your body language, or everyone mimic the body language of the speaker. Maybe you want to exaggerate *fear* or *nervousness* by talking at triple pace or as s-l-o-w-l-y a-s p-o-s-s-i-b-l-e. Try playing the scene *silently,* while exaggerating movements and emotions. Have all the characters "freeze" at a certain point in the scene while you describe in *minute detail* all the things you have been thinking and not saying.

Work through the remaining Steps using improvisation and surprise to vary the revised scripts. Take risks. Have fun!

The Cold Hotdog Syndrome: Reparenting With Humor (Creative Action Routines, Tool III)

When I began to focus on my own needs in recovery, I found I didn't know what my needs were. I had to start somewhere so I decided to focus on the basics — food, clothing and shelter.

I had clothes and shelter, and I had *food,* but I noticed that if there was no one else in front of me who was hungry, I had a hard time eating. I literally could not bring myself to make something to eat. Opening a can of soup and heating it up on the stove was too hard. After all, I might have to add water and stir. This was definitely too much. I began to look at this behavior pattern as probably a good place to start in my reparenting program.

I began observing myself. I noticed that if I were hungry and alone, I would go to the refrigerator and pull out a cold hotdog and just stand there and eat it, while gazing into the nearly empty refrigerator and looking at the things I didn't feel like fixing for myself. A cold hotdog or *two* became my lunch and dinner on some days.

I decided to take this information *out of context* and see what happened. I imagined that a friend called and said, "Hi! I'm in the neighborhood and want to stop by and see you. And by the way, I'm really hungry. Do you have anything to eat?"

Now, if this were *really happening,* I'm sure that I could get creative and fix something substantial. I would even be concerned about it being a balanced meal. I probably would race to the store, if need be, to make sure that my friend had a decent meal.

I again ran through this sequence in my mind, only *this time* to get a different perspective, I decided to treat my friend just the way I treat myself. I imagined my friend visiting and saying, "Oh, by the way, I'm really hungry. Do you have anything I could eat?"

I then visualized myself opening the refrigerator, pulling out a cold hotdog, handing it to her with no bun — no nothing and saying, "Sure. Here you go!"

When I took this issue of mine and developed it in this context, it became funny because of the element of surprise. Who would expect someone to offer a guest a cold hotdog right from the fridge?

This approach also exaggerates the behavior so that it becomes clearer to me how I am treating myself, in contrast to how I treat others. I had also managed to "lighten up" the issue for myself by laughing about it (instead of judging myself). From this lighter perspective, it was easy to see a way to creatively change my behavior. I decided to treat myself more like a guest!

As a reparenting exercise, I now began pretending that there was a small child seated at my table saying, "I'm hungry! Will you fix me something to eat?"

I *would* and I encouraged myself to go ahead with pretending it was for *someone else* for as long as I needed to. This seemed to make it okay for me to go to the trouble of preparing a meal. When I sat down to eat, I thanked myself for the food I had prepared. Both parts of me (the Child that needed to eat and the Adult who fixed the food) seem happier — *and better fed!*

It really didn't take many times of pretending I was fixing food for someone else before I was able to prepare food for myself. I've begun eating in a way that feels good to me, most of the time. This is how I personally beat the dreaded Cold Hotdog Syndrome.

One additional benefit that unexpectedly came of this process was an ability to look at how I'd learned to deny myself good food and care in my childhood dysfunctional home. My family had often been very poor, and as the older girl, I would have to prepare the food and really make it *stretch*. These sorts of memories can be very painful and difficult for me to see; but, with this lighter outlook, I can add this information to my Fourth Step inventory.

The Cold Hotdog Syndrome Exercises

Check the basics — food, clothing and shelter — in your own life, and notice if there are areas of your own needs where you hand yourself a cold hotdog instead of the care you'd expect to give a friend who is your guest. How do you feel about these cold hotdog areas, when you think about them without attempting to introduce humor?

Look over the Introducing Humor section in Tool III, and try some of the suggestions. Pretend you have a job as writer for a stand-up comedian and are using this basic need as a way to put together a really great script. Or, pretend you're writing about *somebody else* who has these funny ways of taking care of herself. Do what it takes to "lighten up" and to stop judging for awhile!

Share your script with a trusted individual or group. Is it okay for *them* to laugh? Is it okay for *you* to laugh? *(Step 5)*

As your own loving parent experiment with treating yourself like a guest and notice how and if it works for you. It's perfectly okay to go on giving yourself cold hotdogs if you like. It's entirely up to you! *(Steps 9 and 6)*

After some time has elapsed, come back to your script and other notes on this process and notice any insights from your childhood experiences that influenced you. Notice any feelings *under* the humor, associated with these past experiences. Is there sadness, anger or shame? Note these insights and feelings in your Fourth Step, if you hadn't observed them before.

A Friend's Reflection Exercise
(Adapting A Creative Action Routine, Tool III)

Follow these steps:

1. Stand facing a partner, with about four feet between

you, so that there is enough room for each to move
comfortably, without bumping into things. One
person agrees to be the *leader,* the other, the *follower,*
to begin this process.

2. The leader stands naturally. The follower takes a few
minutes to study the leader; then she or he attempts to
duplicate exactly everything about the leader, using
her or his own body as though it were a mirror (in
reflection).

3. As the leader, watch carefully. What do you notice
about yourself in what is being reflected? If you think
the follower is not quite accurate, give her or him
feedback. Because it's not easy to mimic exactly, take
all the time you need to develop communication and
feedback between the players in this Exercise. Often
the leader's body language or postures she or he
hadn't been aware of previously become revealed in
this friend's reflection.

4. Try saying a few things about yourself or changing
your position, while the follower moves to reflect you.
Continue for about five minutes.

5. Then trade roles. Try acting out a *feeling* while being
reflected. Reflect each other's *walk* or other behaviors.
Make sure you allow time for feedback from each
other. Give yourself feedback, too. See this as a Step 10
inventory.

   Make notes which include:

   • What you saw
   • Emotions you felt
   • What thoughts you had
   • What memories you experienced
   • Your body sensations

A big part of recovery is seeing yourself and allowing others
to see you. Use this exercise as a *physical* way to do some
Fourth or Tenth Step inventories, and allow your sharing to be
a form of Fifth Step with a trusted friend or sponsor.

Sharing Held Feelings

Acknowledgment and thanks go to *Candice D.* for this exercise, which is designed to strengthen the bond of intimacy through facilitating honesty in conflict or critical feedback situations.

In working Steps 8 and 9, this structured approach to communication may be a big help, especially where old, established patterns of "stuffing" feelings are being challenged. This structure is also a useful Creative Action Routine and a practical way to apply the Freedom Wheel's integrity/ assertiveness spokes in potential conflicts *(Steps 10 and 12)*.

1. First, get in touch with how you are feeling. This may not be easy. You may encounter *denial* mechanisms in yourself that serve to mask, rationalize or minimize your feelings and/or your value (importance) in the situation or relationship.

   Example: In a shared housing arrangement, Inez was bothered by her roommate Barbara's habit of leaving dishes and cups in the common rooms and areas. Inez called what she was feeling bothered because she didn't like to think of herself as being angry. Anger reminded Inez of her parents shouting at each other and even becoming violent. She didn't feel like that (although she sometimes *did* have a *fantasy* of throwing all those spaghetti-crusted plates off the deck). Instead of thinking of herself as angry, she *masked* her feeling by giving it a less specific name. She also may have *minimized* if she told herself, "At least my bedroom and the garage don't have slimy cups!" or *rationalized* by thinking, "Other people have different lifestyles, after all." (Either of these last two statements may be true, but they still have nothing to do with how Inez is feeling about her roommate!)

2. After you have admitted to yourself your feelings in the situation or relationship, ask yourself if you want to share this feeling with the person(s) in question. Many of us have been conditioned to feel *compelled* to

share, without reserving the right and power to ourselves to decide who we will allow into intimacy with us by exposing our feelings and thoughts to them.

Example: Inez may decide she would rather replace Barbara (if Inez is the leaseholder) or move herself. Is it *worth working out,* from Inez's point of view? This is a question for Inez to answer, taking into account such factors as shared financial responsibilities perform-ance, other fun-time activities and whatever else she chooses to consider.

3. If you decide you wish to strengthen the bonds of intimacy with the person involved you may wish to prepare the interaction by asking her if she is willing to receive *held feelings* you have for her. This is an optional part of this process. If you are feeling something very strongly, you may wish to omit this step and just go on to the next one.

Example: Inez decides she wants to work out this issue because she likes a lot about Barbara and enjoys living with her. Inez has not communicated about this matter before and decides to use this step to open this level of communication involving *critical feedback.* Because Barbara hasn't read this workbook (as far as Inez knows), Inez uses words Barbara can understand, "I have some critical feedback for you, Barbara. Are you in a space to receive it now?"

4. If the above step is used and the other person is feeling strong enough or has time to receive your held feelings, express them, as clearly and as concretely as possible. Address the behavior the other person and your feeling response. (If the other person isn't willing to receive your held feeling *now,* make a definite time in the not too distant future when she will be willing, or determine if she is not willing.)

Example: "Barbara, when you leave your dishes and cups around the house, I feel angry."

5. If you feel safe enough to do so, add some informa-tion about your own background and history that

contributes to your feeling. However, be careful not to minimize, rationalize or mask your honest feeling response to the behavior under discussion. Share information that can aid the other person in seeing your point of view.

Example: "I feel angry because I end up picking up after you, and that isn't okay with me. I feel safer and more comfortable in my home when it's not cluttered. Besides, I don't like the smell of dirty dishes!"

6. You may have a solution to offer. Or you may specifically request that the other person do or cease doing a behavior. If you have a preference, communicate it.

   Example: "I've gotten this flat basket out of the garage, and I'm going to put it here by the couch. I would like you to agree to put your dishes into it and then carry it in to the dishwasher when the basket gets full or before it gets smelly!"

7. You also have the option to include some strokes for the person, as long as you stick to being honest and aren't losing the focus of communication at issue. If it feels appropriate, you may wish to share some of your good feelings, which may also fall into the category of held feelings.

   Example: "There's so much about our relationship that I truly value; I want to work this out with you. You're a really responsible roommate when it comes to sharing the phone and the bathroom. You're a cheerful person, too, Barbara, and it's a real pleasure to share time with you!"

Healing Through Recreation (Exercise In Loving, Caring For And Respecting The Inner Child)

Our thanks for this exercise go to *Dave L.,* who describes himself as "an Adult Child learning to reparent himself by utilizing recreation."

"Learning to reparent ourselves with gentleness, humor and

love can take place in all areas of our lives. Recreation, the adult word for play, can be a good place to begin reparenting because it allows us to contact the Inner Child through play. By learning to play in ways that demonstrate love, care and respect for the Inner Child, we begin to supply our own reparenting and begin to take responsibility for our own life. In fact, the recognition of need for recreation is an initial step in taking care of the Inner Child. This step helps relieve us of ~ompulsive behavior, such as workaholism.

"Having been raised in an alcoholic and workaholic family, I had little or no understanding of the need and benefits of recreation. As part of my own recovery process, I began to explore integrating regular recreation into my life. Initially, I approached recreation in the compulsive way that I had learned to approach life. Gradually, I learned to treat myself with loving kindness and to recreate in noncompulsive ways. Learning to take responsibility for my life, becoming an actor rather than a reactor and letting go of the addiction to excitement were some of the benefits of my new approach. I found that backpacking as a form of recreation was a metaphor for becoming a responsible actor in my own life.

"Listening to the Inner Child was what brought me to backpacking. As I overcame the effects of denial, good and bad, memories of my childhood began to come into consciousness. I recalled the sense of wholeness, joy and safety that I had as a child when I hiked and explored the fields, forests and streams where we lived. I sensed that those feelings of wholeness, joy and safety could return in my life if I gave that Inner Child the opportunity to reexperience nature in that fashion. I also experienced my feelings of being unable to take care of myself, helpless, defenseless and afraid of the dark.

Accepting the validity of both sets of feelings was the first step in reparenting the Inner Child. How could I assist the Inner Child in alleviating his fears so that he could experience the positive feelings that were just on the other side of the fears? How would a loving, caring, respecting parent assist his child in this process? The first stage for me was recognition and acceptance of all my feelings, not denying them. The second, was allowing myself the opportunity to experience all of my feelings, in a safe and secure nonjudgmental environment. Gathering information about my chosen form of recreation was the third part in the process for me. Making decisions based on what I had learned was the fourth part, and the fifth was acting based on the feelings, information and decisions.

"Each of the steps is described in greater detail below. As in any Adult Children process the caveat, 'Take what you want and leave the rest,' is appropriate."

Stage I: Identify Potential Recreational Opportunities

Take some quiet time and recall what positive memories of childhood you may possess. What was most fun for *you*? What brought you joy and happiness? If you cannot remember, talk to someone who knew you when you were young and ask him what brought you joy and provided happiness. Oftentimes, your own memory will be stimulated by the discussions. Once you identify an activity that you enjoyed as a child, ask yourself if you could enjoy that activity now. You may remember several things before you find one that feels good for you now. Give yourself an opportunity to experience the positive feelings that you once had about that activity. Examine how you feel about that activity now. Sadness, fear, guilt, anger or other feelings that are often difficult for Adult Children to experience, may arise.

Stage II: Experience All Your Feelings About The Activity

An essential part of Stage II is giving yourself the opportunity to experience all of your feelings about the activity selected by your Inner Child in a nonjudgmental and accepting way. Love yourself for the courage to look, even if what you find doesn't feel good. Experiencing the feelings that do not feel good will release your creativity and provide the motivation to continue this loving and caring activity. Be aware of any self-critical attitudes that may creep into this process and lovingly accept this criticism and let it go. You may want to share these feelings with someone you trust, such as a sponsor or a good friend. If, at this point you feel that the activity you have selected is not appropriate for you, choose another that seems more workable and continue with Stage II.

Stage III: Gather Information About The Activity

Gathering information about your selected activity is the third step in this healing through recreational exercise. Some ideas regarding the information you need to gather can result from asking yourself, "How would a loving, caring, respectful parent introduce a child to this activity?" Other questions may include, "Where are you going?" "Who are you going with?" "How are you getting there and returning?" "Do you have the resources necessary to take care of yourself when you arrive, such as money, equipment, knowledge, experience and friends?" "When will you return?" "Have you considered how to deal with unexpected occurrences?"

Many of us received these types of questions in our childhood from parents who were fearful, and we often felt their fear rather than their concern. Others of us had parents who were not concerned at all with these issues. Resistance to answering these questions may arise as a result of this old conditioning. However, remember that you are a loving, caring parent concerned with your Inner Child's safety **and** his ability to have fun and grow. If you undertake to answer these questions in a spirit of fun and growth, much joy can be obtained.

Stage IV: Make Decisions About The Activity

Evaluating your answers to the questions in Stage III and making decisions comprise Stage IV. Keeping in mind that you are acting as a loving parent to your Inner Child, decide which activity is best for you, what resources you will need, whether to go alone or with others, what you will need to learn and how you will deal with unexpected occurrences. While evaluating the activity and making decisions, remain open to your feelings about the activity, yourself and the process. Many Adult Children feel bored with this part of the process, often because the excitement of the chaos in the family is not present. Some resist because the process is not spontaneous (another variation of the boredom complaint). Fear, anxiety, helplessness, excitement, joy and sadness may also result. Allow all these feelings and any others to exist and make a commitment to your Inner Child to complete the process. Avoidance at this point is very common; it reflects the avoidance of loving adult behaviors in the alcoholic family. By examining the feelings that arise, an Adult Child can begin to understand where these feelings originated and make the decision to act in responsible and loving ways to the Inner Child.

Stage V: Acting

Acting, doing and participating are involved in the next stage of this healing process. Again, while participating in your chosen recreational activity, maintain a close watch on your feelings. Reevaluate your chosen activity, gather new information about it through participation, reassess your decision (if necessary) and act again. **Above all else, love yourself and learn and enjoy from the process.**

Another Way To View Myself:
An Exercise Using Visualization

The 12 Steps of Recovery are not rigid structures that I need to push myself through, hoping that the form of my "self" will somehow make all the correct compromises. Nor will I come out an acceptable product of recovery on the other end, like some nicely machined devise. Perhaps some of us may have come to see ourselves as products or results of our experiences in school or with authority figures who only wanted us to *perform*. Through the 12 Steps, which are well-suited to support *human* recovery, we can reparent, allow and even encourage ourselves to emerge as unique human beings. A creative way to work the Steps is to use Stage II of the Visualization process to locate and to identify my "self" (with *my* needs and preferences), and to create a structure from my personal interpretation of the 12 Steps that can support me today.

To foster the ability to *symbolically* hold yourself in your hand and to look at yourself, use the following Visualization exercise:

Moving from your favorite place, without any restraints whatsoever, ask your Inner Child to become your guide and to *visualize freely* all the ways he sees your "self." He is free to be as silly and as wild as he likes! Ask your Inner Child, "What form does my 'self' take, in its wholeness?" Without any judgment or restraints allow yourself to become entirely open to the images you discover. Over a period of time, your Inner Child's imagination will begin to *trust* and *communicate* with you in powerful ways.

It makes a difference how you see yourself. How *personally* you are able to adapt the 12 Steps depends on how clearly you come to know your own needs, preferences and inner directions.

Example: If I have discovered that I am a flowing river, I may want to use the Steps as my "banks" or the structure to contain me and give me direction. However, if I have discovered that I am a seedling who is rapidly becoming root-bound in a small pot, I may need to use the Steps as a rich, fertile open field with the soil of new concepts that will allow me to develop my latent potentials. If this river and this seedling are seen as representing two different individuals, it becomes beneficial to use the Steps from quite different perspectives.

Perhaps I am a 1953 Chevy truck, but my mother always saw me as a 1968 MGB sports car, painted fire-engine red! Perhaps I internalized my mother's image of me, and I've always wondered what's wrong with me. For example, don't I enjoy winding out my gears on a racetrack with Triumph Spitfires flying past me, spraying gravel on my windshield?

Perhaps the problem is that I haven't taken the opportunity to get outside myself far enough to notice my bumper sticker that says, *"I'd rather be on a country road!"* — maybe transporting a load of hay to a freshly painted barn. I may have a *vague* sort of feeling that my life isn't quite as it might be; but if I used higher octane fuel or maybe dual carburetors, and just charge on down what feels and looks like the *fast lane* to me, maybe somehow I can win. Most of the problem here appears to be that I don't know or see my own real "self". I may find that I have been looking at a "self" concept that is *separate* from me, further alienating myself from my "self" (while all those gravel pits accumulate in my windshield).

If this technique of applying metaphor in Visualization is unfamiliar to you, try looking over the behaviors on the Victim Roles and Freedom Wheels. Begin identifying your behaviors and attitudes in more conventional terms. Then read over the "Introducing Humor" section of Creative Action Routines, and experiment with "lightening up" insights that come to you about who, what and where you are or have been in your own life. Your Inner Child is certain to thank you!

Take Yourself Literally: Creative Action In The Physical World

If you feel like you're a mess, look around your environment and see if there's a mess you can straighten or clean. If you're feeling too rigid or structured in your thinking or feeling responses, check your home, your room or your desk. Do any of these areas reflect these conditions? Is *everything* exactly arranged, just so? Try loosening up somewhere, in whichever of these areas you choose, and notice how you *feel* as a result or while you're doing it.

For example, once in prayer, I was asking for what I called "clarity of vision", or help in seeing a clear view for myself, a larger, more expansive view of my whole reality. While I prayed an Inner voice responded, "If you want *clarity of vision,* why don't you start by *washing your windows?*" (God, as I understand God, has a sense of humor!) So, I actually got up and washed my windows. Just loosening up mentally and emotionally, combined with getting active physically, served to get my imagination opened too, and I certainly did have clarity of vision with my windows unsmudged.

I focused on the view outside the kitchen windows, and I drank in the beauty of the turning colors of early autumn's "Indian Summer", my favorite season. I watched the liquid amber tree surrender in rich colors to the winds of fall, painting a new face on the hillside beyond. This ritual comforted me as I also surrendered to the seasons.

Making Reasonable Commitments
Self-Assessment Inventory Exercise

1. What commitment would I like to make to myself, as a part of my recovery at this time?
2. Is this a commitment I *really want* to keep? (Be honest! If you are making a commitment you think you should keep, but you really have no desire to do so, the chances are pretty great that you won't keep it.)
3. What is a *reasonable* time frame (my time frame) in which to accomplish this? (Start small!)

   Example: Don't commit to meditating for 30 minutes each day from now until eternity. This is not reasonable. You might start with 10 minutes per day, for three times in the next week. Or try five minutes just for today, or whatever you feel sure you can do.
4. How will I know when I've accomplished this? Is it *measurable?* (In the example or meditation, it would be obvious to see if you've done what you committed to do. But, what about the sorts of commitments that are more general?)

   Example: "I'm going to experience 'more' joy in my life, or 'less' stress." These sorts of commitments will be difficult to gauge. Be as specific as possible and find ways to measure your success.
5. Have I set this commitment up in a way that feels good to me, and in a way I'm certain I can accomplish it? (If not, rework it! You may be setting yourself up for failure.)
6. What if I'm not able to keep my commitment? (Be easy on yourself. Another aspect of keeping commitments is to experience *not* keeping commitments. You might ask yourself: "What got in my way? What did I do, instead? Was my commitment a *reasonable* one?" These may be clues to your patterns, reflecting on how you operate in your life in a more general way.)

7. Do I *want* to recommit to this goal? (If it worked well and made you feel good, you may want to recommit to it exactly as before. If not, rework it. Try something else. Or don't make any commitments for a week. The choice is yours.)

Affirmation Dramas

This technique is an application of Role Playing from Creative Action Routines, Tool III, which was developed for use in workshops. It can also be done as a Guided Visualization/Active Imagination process.

1. Remember a scene involving you relating to other people. Choose a scene that didn't come out the way you wanted — one where you lost out, felt sad or hurt, or were the victim. If you have difficulty recalling material, review your past with the Victim Roles Wheel, Tool I. Reflecting on interactions you have experienced in family, business or social life.

2. Rewrite the scene, imagining it just *exactly* as you would have liked it to have developed or turned out. Put in dialogue, actions and facial expressions to make it become entirely real to you. In this scene of re-enactment try to build your sense of self-worth and to give yourself whatever attention, care or acknowledgment you desired.

3. From the co-participants in the workshop or support group select those you feel are best suited to play the various roles. Ask them if they are willing to be those characters for you. If they are comfortable in the roles offered, explain the action along with any dialogue, expressions or behaviors you would like them to include.

4. Go ahead and experience this **affirmation drama**. Give yourself permission to experience the satisfaction, happiness or success you wanted in this situation before, but could not obtain. Now that you have it, *bask in it.* Ask your Inner Child to accept this

experience as a form of amends *(Step 9)*.

Note: If you are doing this exercise as a Guided Visualization experience, remember to expand your imagination to include spiritual aid, allies or whatever you are inspired to offer to your Inner Child to make this experience deeply satisfying. In either application, **you run the show. Create yourself satisfied!**

11 BURNOUT, DISILLUSIONMENT AND LOSS OF INTEREST

Denial has many facets. Rejecting or discrediting exactly what might prove most helpful to us and becoming distracted, unfocused or just too tired to go on are all ways internal denial can seek to restore us to former habits and lifestyles. Old ways die hard!

Objectively, in any support group that does not limit its membership there are likely to be personalities who project authority or dependence roles on us. There are rebels who will cross talk no matter what the rules say, and there are self-appointed monitors of everybody's conduct who are smugly assured of the backing of the group.

Support groups reflect all the types of personalities that result from growing up in alcoholic and/or dysfunctional homes. It's almost certain that someone will remind us of a childhood role model, tormentor or ally, whether it be in what he says, how he says it, or by his style and body language. Coping with projection in Adult Children support groups can pose a real challenge!

Conscientious as most 12-Step program support groups are regarding anonymity, cross talk and discouragement of gossip or confrontations among members, it is still possible for trust and confidence to be bruised.

Disillusioned, some Adult Children may take old paths of retreat. Alternatives to this self-abandonment include changing support groups or days of attendance to avoid crossing paths with particular individuals. A course of greater personal challenge rests in seeking to use abrasion as an incentive to work the Step 10 *and* the Step 4 inventories while endeavoring to see *both* the nature of the current issues *and* their inceptive roots in childhood experience and trauma. Each individual must gauge her own personal needs in each situation and suit her conduct to best support her own recovery and goals.

A good general rule is to make another six meetings (not necessarily at the same group or meeting) if an upset or personal disillusionment occurs. This assures that a more balanced view and settled emotional state will have time and opportunity to prevail over old crisis-centered patterns, which may be among the most insidious forms of internal denial.

Of course, every person has the right to expect safety, confidentiality and unqualified acceptance in a 12-Step support group, and no one is asked to put up with incivility or aggression. Most groups have clear guidelines that protect the meetings and meeting places from disruption. As individuals make personal progress in recovery, it stands to reason that support groups tend to become healthier, clearer and more balanced over a period of time. Participation in support groups remains a voluntary, individual choice. It's a good idea to periodically reconsider the role support groups play and just what commitment is appropriate for you.

As one member, **Patruska B.,** stated, "Only *you* know what comes back to you when you say the Serenity Prayer — what to 'accept', what to 'change'."

Building Self-Esteem In My Recovery/Discovery Today

Build Self-Esteem by living this *one day* as well as I know how!

Build Self-Esteem by *giving myself credit* where due and earned (whether or not anyone else does).

Build Self-Esteem by actually *getting interested in feedback,* being a secure enough person today, not a "house of cards" that might collapse in a slight wind!

Build Self-Esteem by doing *secret favors* and never letting it be known by anyone but me.

Build Self-Esteem by not proving anything to challengers who aren't interested in sticking to the point, for whatever reasons. (*Challenging,* after all, is a form of manipulation, unless an honest search for answers is involved.)

Build Self-Esteem by treating all my personal resources with respect. If I've been "throwing myself away" in any area of my life: health, finances, time or energy, **just for today,** I'll remind myself that everything about *me* is worthy of my care and my respect!

My Personal Affirmations

My Personal Affirmations

My Personal Affirmations

My Personal Goals

My Personal Goals

My Personal Achievements

My Personal Achievements

More Helpful 12-Step Books

HEALING A BROKEN HEART:
12 Steps of Recovery for Adult Children
Kathleen W.

This useful 12-Step book is presently the number one resource for all Adult Children support groups.

ISBN 0-932194-65-6 $7.95

12 STEPS TO SELF-PARENTING For Adult Children
Philip Oliver-Diaz and Patricia A. O'Gorman

This gentle 12-Step guide takes the reader from pain to healing and self-parenting, from anger to forgiveness, and from fear and despair to recovery.

ISBN 0-932194-68-0 $7.95

THE 12-STEP BOOKLETS
Mary M. McKee

Each beautifully illustrated booklet deals with a step, using a story from nature in parable form. The 12 booklets (one for each step) lead us to a better understanding of ourselves.

ISBN 1-55874-002-3 $8.95

UNDERSTANDING ME: Your Personal Story
Sharon Wegscheider-Cruse

This workbook shows the reader how to compile a three-generational family history and how to use the material to reshape the future.

ISBN 0-932194-29-X $13.95

GIFTS FOR PERSONAL GROWTH & RECOVERY
Wayne Kritsberg

A goldmine of positive techniques for recovery (affirmations, journal writing, visualizations, guided meditations, etc.), this book is indispensable for those seeking personal growth.

ISBN 0-932194-60-5 $6.95

Other Books By . . .

HEALTH COMMUNICATIONS, INC.

Enterprise Center
3201 Southwest 15th Street
Deerfield Beach, FL 33442
Phone: 800-851-9100

ADULT CHILDREN OF ALCOHOLICS
Janet Woititz
Over a year on The New York Times Best Seller list,this book is the primer
on Adult Children of Alcoholics.
ISBN 0-932194-15-X   **$6.95**

STRUGGLE FOR INTIMACY
Janet Woititz
Another best seller, this book gives insightful advice on learning to love
more fully.
ISBN 0-932194-25-7   **$6.95**

DAILY AFFIRMATIONS: For Adult Children of Alcoholics
Rokelle Lerner
These positive affirmations for every day of the year paint a mental picture
of your life as you choose it to be.
ISBN 0-932194-27-3   **$6.95**

*CHOICEMAKING: For Co-dependents, Adult Children and Spirituality
Seekers* — Sharon Wegscheider-Cruse
This useful book defines the problems and solves them in a positive way.
ISBN 0-932194-26-5   **$9.95**

LEARNING TO LOVE YOURSELF: Finding Your Self-Worth
Sharon Wegscheider-Cruse
"Self-worth is a choice, not a birthright", says the author as she shows us
how we can choose positive self-esteem.
ISBN 0-932194-39-7   **$7.95**

LET GO AND GROW: Recovery for Adult Children
Robert Ackerman
An in-depth study of the different characteristics of adult children of
alcoholics with guidelines for recovery.
ISBN 0-932194-51-6   **$8.95**

LOST IN THE SHUFFLE: The Co-dependent Reality
Robert Subby
A look at the unreal rules the co-dependent lives by and the way out of the
dis-eased reality.
ISBN 0-932194-45-1   **$8.95**

New Books . . .
from Health Communications

BRADSHAW ON: THE FAMILY: A Revolutionary Way of Self-Discovery
John Bradshaw
The host of the nationally televised series of the same name shows us how families can be healed and we as individuals can realize our full potential.
ISBN 0-932194-54-0   **$9.95**

HEALING THE CHILD WITHIN: Discovery and recovery for Adult Children of Dysfunctional Families — Charles Whitfield
Dr. Whitfield defines, describes and discovers how we can reach our Child Within to heal and nurture our woundedness.
ISBN 0-932194-40-0   **$8.95**

WHISKY'S SONG: An Explicit Story of Surviving in an Alcoholic Home
Mitzi Chandler
A beautiful but brutal story of growing up where violence and neglect are everyday occurrences conveys a positive message of survival and love.
ISBN 0-932194-42-7   **$6.95**

New Books on Spiritual Recovery . . .
from Health Communications

THE JOURNEY WITHIN: A Spiritual Path to Recovery
Ruth Fishel
This book will lead you from your dysfunctional beginnings to the place within where renewal occurs.
ISBN 0-932194-41-9   **$8.95**

LEARNING TO LIVE IN THE NOW: 6-Week Personal Plan To Recovery
Ruth Fishel
The author gently introduces you to the valuable healing tools of meditation, positive creative visualization and affirmations.
ISBN 0-932194-62-1   **$7.95**

GENESIS: Spirituality in Recovery for Co-dependents
by Julie D. Bowden and Herbert L. Gravitz
A self-help spiritual program for adult children of trauma, an in-depth look at "turning it over" and "letting go".
ISBN 0-932194-56-7   **$6.95**

GIFTS FOR PERSONAL GROWTH AND RECOVERY
Wayne Kritsberg
Gifts for healing which include journal writing, breathing, positioning and meditation.
ISBN 0-932194-60-5   **$6.95**

Books from . . .
Health Communications

THIRTY-TWO ELEPHANT REMINDERS: A Book of Healthy Rules
Mary M. McKee
Concise advice by 32 wise elephants whose wit and good humor will also
be appearing in a 12-step calendar and greeting cards.
ISBN 0-932194-59-1 $3.95

BREAKING THE CYCLE OF ADDICTION: For Adult Children of Alcoholics
Patricia O'Gorman and Philip Oliver-Diaz
For parents who were raised in addicted families, this guide teaches you
about Breaking the Cycle of Addiction from *your* parents to your children.
Must reading for any parent.
ISBN 0-932194-37-0 $8.95

AFTER THE TEARS: Reclaiming The Personal Losses of Childhood
Jane Middelton-Moz and Lorie Dwinnel
Your lost childhood must be grieved in order for you to recapture your
self-worth and enjoyment of life. This book will show you how.
ISBN 0-932194-36-2 $7.95

ADULT CHILDREN OF ALCOHOLICS SYNDROME: From Discovery to Recovery
Wayne Kritsberg
Through the Family Integration System and foundations for healing the
wounds of an alcoholic-influenced childhood are laid in this important
book.
ISBN 0-932194-30-3 $7.95

OTHERWISE PERFECT: People and Their Problems with Weight
Mary S. Stuart and Lynnzy Orr
This book deals with all the varieties of eating disorders, from anorexia to
obesity, and how to cope sensibly and successfully.
ISBN 0-932194-57-5 $7.95

Orders must be prepaid by check, money order, MasterCard or Visa.
Purchase orders from agencies accepted (attach P.O. documentation)
for billing. Net 30 days.
Minimum shipping/handling — $1.25 for orders less than $25. For
orders over $25, add 5% of total for shipping and handling. Florida
residents add 5% sales tax.

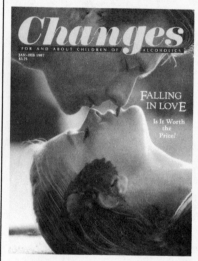